IMPROVE YOUR MEMORY SKILLS

Francis S. Bellezza is a professor of psychology at Ohio University. He has written many articles on human learning and memory that have appeared in psychological and educational journals.

Francis S. Bellezza

IMPROVE YOUR MEMORY SKILLS

A SPECTRUM BOOK

Prentice-Hall, Inc., Englewood Cliffs, New Jersey 07632

Library of Congress Cataloging in Publication Data

Bellezza, Francis S.
    Improve your memory skills.

    "A Spectrum Book."
    Bibliography: p.
    Includes index.
    1. Mnemonics.   I. Title.
BF385.B45   153.1'4   82-5396
ISBN 0-13-453316-X   AACR2
ISBN 0-13-453308-9 (pbk.)

This Spectrum Book can be made available to businesses
and organizations at a special discount when ordered in
large quantities. For more information, contact:
Prentice-Hall, Inc., General Publishing Division,
Special Sales, Englewood Cliffs, New Jersey 07632.

1 2 3 4 5 6 7 8 9 10

ISBN 0-13-453316-X

ISBN 0-13-453308-9 {PBK.}

Editorial/production supervision by Rita Young
Cover illustration by April Blair Stewart
Manufacturing buyer: Cathie Lenard

Prentice-Hall International, Inc., *London*
Prentice-Hall of Australia Pty. Limited, *Sydney*
Prentice-Hall Canada Inc., *Toronto*
Prentice-Hall of India Private Limited, *New Delhi*
Prentice-Hall of Japan, Inc., *Tokyo*
Prentice-Hall of Southeast Asia Pte. Ltd., *Singapore*
Whitehall Books Limited, *Wellington, New Zealand*

to my wife, Suzanne

Contents

IMPROVE YOUR MEMORY SKILLS

chapter one

Introduction

For the last few years I have taught a course to college students that deals with the improvement of memory skills. During the course many of the students have reported the successful use of the techniques in their class work. Most of them believed that these memorizing techniques would be of help to them in their personal, academic, and professional lives. There is nothing secret or magical about these memory procedures. Mnemonic (knee-MON-ik) techniques have been around for hundreds of years and date back to the ancient Greek and Roman cultures. Mnemonic techniques are special methods of memorizing that ensure that large amounts of information can be remembered for a relatively long period of time.

I believe that mnemonic techniques are not in more general use for two main reasons: (1) their method of use must be clearly understood before they can be used effectively; and (2) the mnemonics that are potentially the most useful require a fair amount of practice before they become efficient means of memorization. In this book I have tried to explain the use of each technique as clearly and as completely as possible. I have also tried to give complete examples of the use of each technique. My goal was to make it clear how each mnemonic should be used. The problem of obtaining an adequate amount of practice is a major one and one that you, as the aspiring mnemonist, must deal with. Knowing how to do something in the sense of describing what steps should be taken is not the same as being able to use the procedure successfully. In this book a number of exercises are provided as each technique is discussed. The technique can be mastered better by working through these exercises. Sometimes you will have to do only a few exercises before feeling confident about using some mnemonic procedure; other times you may do all the exercises and still not feel confident. In those cases you will have to go back and review. For some of the more difficult exercises I have provided example solutions which can be found at the back of the book. These solutions suggest how the material presented for memorization can be dealt with. Every exercise with an asterisk (*) preceding it has a sample solution provided. I hope that these suggestions will provide some insight for those of you who have problems mastering the various techniques.

Why memorize?

You probably believe that having a good memory is important or else you wouldn't be looking at this book. However, "memorizing," that is, trying to intentionally remember large amounts of information, is considered by most of us in this age as being the wrong way to deal with new information and new experiences. What we believe we should do is comprehend and relate to what we are experiencing. Insight and understanding are more important than memorization. Nobody wants to return to the days when children sat in school rooms reciting over and over again things that they didn't understand, that they had to commit to memory. But perhaps our ideas have moved too far in this direction. Ask any group of college students and they will tell you that in many college courses understanding is not enough; you must also remember details if you are to get a good grade. It is important to remember that the glum-looking person with the white wig who is known as "The Father of Our Country" has the name "George Washington." Furthermore, memorizing is not limited to the special world of college campuses. Would you like to go to a physician and be told that he knew what disease you had but couldn't remember its name? What about hiring someone to write reports who is intelligent, understands what is happening, but can't remember how to correctly spell words? How about remembering faces and names? Many professional individuals whose jobs depend on meeting and remembering the names of countless people do not feel that it is appropriate to say, "I understood what you were saying to me the last time we met, but I cannot remember your name."

Let's not say that understanding is unimportant; let's say that sometimes remembering is also important. This book is for those who would like to better remember some of the information that they have to deal with everyday and are willing to put some effort into learning procedures that will help them do so.

When memorizing can be helpful

Let's look at two imaginary people and list some of the situations they encounter where memory techniques might be particularly useful. The numbers in parentheses that you will see indicate the chapter in the book that can help in each of these situations. Our first person is Mary Smith, who is a college freshman. As a freshman, Mary lives in a dormitory, but she hopes to join a sorority and live in a sorority house next year. She has met quite a few sorority members during rush and has talked to a few more than once. When she sees them on campus, she says "Hello," but wishes that she could remember their names as well as recognize their faces (Chapter 8). Mary is secretary-treasurer of a campus organization called Environmental Concern. Often she must telephone various officers and members of the club as well as various university officials and other organizations. She has a small notebook with all the telephone numbers carefully written in it, but she sometimes wishes that she didn't have to continue to look up phone numbers that she has already looked up a half-dozen times (Chapter 6). One of the tough courses that Mary has to take is called Overview of World History. The large number of dates that she has to memorize is driving her mad. She thinks that she must repeat the date over and over again until she remembers it. She wishes that there was an easier and more interesting way to remember historic dates (Chapter 6). Mary's course in geography is also causing her some concern. How can she possibly remember the lists of important commercial and agricultural products from each of the countries of Europe (Chapter 7)? Spanish is fun, but memorizing all those new vocabulary words is a bore. Fortunately, there are other ways of remembering new foreign-language vocabulary words than simply writing them over and over (Chapter 6). What about all of the new technical words Mary is running across in her courses? Is there some way to better remember their pronunciation and meaning (Chapter 6)? Just this week Mary had to study for an essay exam in psychology. Her professor is going to ask the class to write an essay on three of the twelve major topics that they have studied and discussed over the last ten weeks, but nobody knows which three topics will be asked for. How should Mary study for this exam? Is there an effective way to organize and remember the important information connected with each topic (Chapter 9)?

I guess that we would all agree that college students should develop good study techniques and that these should include methods for remembering what they study. But are mnemonic techniques helpful to those who are not college students? I think so. Let's take the example of Mary's father, Bill Smith, who is a sales representative for a firm that produces and sells electronic equipment. Bill Smith often meets new people as part of his job, and his success as a salesman depends on remembering the names of these people when he meets them again (Chapter 8). He also tries to remember the changing prices and new model numbers of a large variety of electronic equipment (Chapter 5). He could refer to his catalogues when a customer requests information, but he would much prefer to be able to give this information quickly without thumbing through his books (Chapter 5). Often Bill will have only five or ten minutes to make a few phone calls from an airport or from a hotel. It would be convenient for him if he were able to memorize the area codes and telephone numbers of the people and firms that he frequently has to call (Chapter 6). One Friday, Bill had to give a talk to a sales group on the changes that had taken place since 1970 in the marketing of electronic equipment. He had a nice talk prepared: some good points, some statistics, some good examples, and even a few jokes. He would like to have given the talk without constantly looking at his notes (Chapter 9).

Memory skills are not limited to helping people who are either in school or at work. One day last week Bill was driving along the freeway and thinking about one of his projects at home. He wants to build some cabinets for the recreation room. As he drove along, he planned what he wanted to do and decided on the various materials that he would have to buy at the supply store. Traffic was heavy so he didn't want to stop and write down what he had thought out. He had to hope that he would later remember all the things he had decided to do (Chapter 3).

Some of the memory problems of Bill and Mary Smith are important problems that many of us would like to be able to deal with successfully. If they are, then I can say with some assurance that the techniques discussed in this book will help solve them.

Three basic memory procedures

How do we develop better memories? Should we practice memorizing so that memory gets stronger just as a weight lifter lifts weights to make his muscles stronger? No, this is not the correct approach. To remember better a person must develop memory *skill* not memory *strength.* Memorizing is more like learning to solve a problem than it is like strengthening a muscle. Practice is necessary to better memorize, but it is very important to practice using a specific memory technique. If you do not understand a mnemonic technique or if you are using that mnemonic technique in the wrong way, then your practice may not be worth the time you spend at it. A number of principles of remembering will be discussed throughout the book. However, there are three procedures that play a major role in the various mnemonics to be discussed. They are: (1) the use of memorized *pegs* to which new information can be attached in memory, (2) the use of visual imagery, and (3) the use of substitution techniques to make information that is difficult to remember, such as numbers and abstract words, more easily memorized. These three procedures of *pegging, imagery,* and *substitution* are, perhaps, not more important than some of the other principles of remembering, but they are emphasized here because many people find them strange and somewhat difficult to use at first. Hence, correct use of these three procedures requires a fair amount of practice.

Your memory as a closet

In order to explain how mnemonic techniques work, I would like to introduce the analogy of memory being like a large, floorless closet. Since new information cannot be stacked on the floor of the closet in neat piles as clothing, everything must be attached to pegs on the walls, otherwise the information disappears. Without training in mnemonic techniques our memory closet may have a great deal of wall space but not very many pegs. So one of the tasks ahead will be to create many more pegs to which additional information can be attached whenever necessary. This is the principle of *pegging* and will be discussed in more detail in Chapter 3.

Once the additional pegs have been created, how can we be sure that the information attached to these pegs will remain there for a reasonable amount of time? This is where the principle of *imagery* comes in. The use of visual imagery ensures that information will be securely attached to a peg and remain there until it is later needed and can be *retrieved* (Chapter 2). Visual imagery is like using the loop on an article of clothing to securely attach it to a peg on the wall of the closet. Sometimes, if we start running out of pegs, visual imagery can also be used to attach new information to information already attached to a peg, so that the information that has to be remembered is linked together to form a chain.

The final mnemonic principle that will be emphasized is the use of *substitution* techniques (Chapters 4, 5, and 6). It is not easy to form memorable images of numbers such as 158 or 8536. Also, it is not easy to form images out of meaningful but abstract words such as *advantage* or *method*. Because visual imagery plays such a large role in techniques of memorization, we will discuss ways of substituting other words for abstract information so that visual images can be formed for them, and the abstract information better remembered. Going back to the analogy of memory as a closet and new information as clothing that we want to store in the closet, the abstract numbers and words can be thought of as articles of clothing with no loops on them by which we can attach them to a peg. The substitution techniques are a way of adding a loop so that this information can be stored.

What is not discussed

There are many mnemonic techniques that are not discussed in this book, but most of them are variations of the basic mnemonic procedures that are described here. In the bibliography I have included a list of books and articles on mnemonic devices in which the interested reader can find discussion of other mnemonics. Since the present book concentrates on learning how to use mnemonics, two other aspects of mnemonic devices are completely ignored. One topic concerns the fascinating and important history of mnemonic devices. In the bibliography I have listed books and articles that deal with this history. The other important topic missing from this book, especially from the point of view of my colleagues who are cognitive psychologists, concerns an evaluation of the effectiveness of the various mnemonic techniques based on experimental research. Although there is a large and growing literature dealing with research on mnemonic devices, as yet many basic questions about their relative effectiveness cannot be answered. Also in the bibliography are references to books discussing the research that has been done on mnemonic devices with respect to their effectiveness and their relation to other principles of learning and memory.

chapter two

The use
of visual imagery
in remembering

Many of the words people have to deal with in everyday life represent the names of objects that can be seen, heard, touched,
tasted, or smelled. Long experience with these objects means
that a word such as *apple* can elicit a picture of an apple in our
minds if we concentrate on the word and try to form this mental picture. This mental picture is called a visual image. Many
people experience enough visual imagery to "see" the stem of
the apple and the different shades of red and yellow on its skin.
Some people can mentally "feel" the smooth surface of the skin
of the apple and mentally "hear" the crunch sound an apple
makes when someone bites into it. Some people can imagine
what the apple tastes and smells like. All these imagined sensa-

tions are evidence of mental imagery. Mental imagery, especially visual imagery, will be especially helpful in using the various mnemonic techniques. The more you can get yourself to use visual imagery, the better you will be able to remember information that you want to remember. The purpose of this chapter is to improve your visual imagery skills and to show you how the use of visual imagery relates to remembering.

Try now to form a mental picture of another object, say a dinner plate or something else that you see everyday. Can you mentally see some of the details of its design? Can you mentally see some of its colors? Can you mentally see someone tossing a dinner plate through the air like a Frisbee? If you can visually image detail, color, and interaction, then you have formed a good visual image of the dinner plate.

Form a mental picture of some other common object, such as an automobile. Can you visualize some of its details such as the number of windows, the shape of the front grill, or the switches and meters on the dashboard? What about the car's internal and external colors? Can you see them? Can you "see" the car rolling slowly and bumping into a brick wall?

In order to ensure that you have formed a good visual image of an object, always use the three-point checklist:

1. Can you see some of the *details* of the object?
2. Can you see some of the *color* of the object?
3. Can you see the object in *interaction* with something else?

Exercise 2.1.   The ease of forming clear and vivid visual images of objects improves with practice. Try to form a visual image of each of the following five objects and, using the checklist, take note of their *detail, color,* and *interaction*: a pencil, a television set, a shirt, a dog, a house. Don't stop thinking about the word until you have seen detail, color, and interaction, but not necessarily all at the same time.

No mental imagery?

There are people who insist that even after a great deal of effort they do not experience what is called mental imagery. Perhaps you are one of these people. It is difficult to determine when a person really is or is not experiencing visual imagery, because visual images are private events. It is often difficult to communicate verbally whether or not we are sharing the same mental experiences. However, if you are a person who believes that you are not experiencing the kinds of visual images that have been discussed here, don't be discouraged. If you seem to be a person who thinks entirely in words, then you may do somewhat worse in remembering words representing physical objects, but you may also do somewhat better in remembering abstract words such as *method, glory,* or *benefit* for which visual images are difficult to form.

Here is what you should do when a visual image is requested, but you don't seem to experience a visual image: For example, if the visual image of a pencil is requested, think about a particular pencil and go through the three steps of *detail, color,* and *interaction.* If you don't have a visual image of a pencil, think verbally of some detail of the pencil, such as "a metal band that connects the rubber eraser to the wooden pencil." Next, try to remember the color of the pencil, so you might say to yourself, "The pencil that I am thinking about is yellow." Finally, think of a pencil interacting with something else. For example, you might say to yourself, "Moving a pencil in a circle on a sheet of paper will result in a circle being drawn."

So, in summary, if you think you are a non-visualizer, first try to form a visual image. If you cannot do so, or you don't think you are doing what is being asked for, then form a sentence describing a detail. Next, form a sentence describing the color of the object. Finally, use a sentence to describe the object interacting with something else.

Pairs of words

The basis for many mnemonic techniques is the linking together of pairs of words in memory. Words can be linked in memory by associating the visual images related to these words. Let's take a few examples. Suppose that you were presented with this pair of words: *elephant/cigar*. Instead of forming a visual image of an elephant and then forming a visual image of a cigar, try to form a mental picture that contains both an elephant and a cigar in physical contact or physically interacting in some way. For example, you might form a mental picture of an elephant smoking a cigar, or an elephant picking up a cigar with its trunk, or an elephant stamping out a burning cigar lying on the ground. In each of these images the elephant and the cigar are part of the same mental picture and are interacting in some way. If your mental image seems bizarre or strange, don't worry. You will still remember it; that is the important thing. Once you have formed the mental image, go through the three-point checklist. Can you see some specific detail of both the elephant and the cigar such as the tusks of the elephant and the ash on the end of the cigar? Can you see some color in each object such as the gray of the elephant's skin or the brown tobacco of the cigar? When trying to associate two words using visual imagery, it is not enough to have each one of them in motion. Rather, they should be interacting with one another in some way. Does your visual image for the pair *elephant/cigar* include the elephant vigorously puffing on the cigar, or the cigar going through the air as the elephant lifts it with its trunk, or the elephant's giant foot mashing the burning cigar? Some sort of interaction between the representations of the two words will ensure that they become associated in your memory. Without this interaction the two words will not become integrated and be remembered as a unit.

*Exercise 2.2.   This exercise consists of ten pairs of words. Form a visual image of the objects represented by the words in each pair interacting in some way. Place a check mark in the appropriate column after you take note of the detail, color, and interaction of each image you form. Some of these word combinations may lead to strange and unusual visual images. Don't let that bother you. Use your imagination. Just make sure that the images contain the two objects interacting in some way.

	detail	color	interaction
tree/hammer			
ship/piano			
fork/barrel			
arrow/newspaper			
flag/door			
umbrella/church			
chair/toast			
volcano/harp			
trumpet/flower			
bottle/shoes			

Now, if visual imagery results in good memory, you should be able to remember how the words were paired. The following list consists of the first words from the ten pairs. Look at each word and form a visual image of it. The visual image you experience should be the same image you created when you were studying the pair the word comes from. This means you should be able to easily write down the word that goes with each of the following words without having to look back at the list of pairs. Look at your visual image instead to see what objects are depicted there. By taking note of the detail, color, and interaction, you have fixed the image in your memory.

arrow/_____
chair/_____
bottle/_____
fork/_____
tree/_____
umbrella/_____
volcano/_____
ship/_____
flag/_____
trumpet/_____

If you believe that you are a person who has trouble forming visual images, then you may use verbal descriptions instead. To check detail, describe in words a detail of the object each word in the pair represents. To check color, describe the color of each object. Finally, to check interaction, form a sentence describing the objects interacting in a meaningful way. The sentence you form may be unusual, but it should be meaningful, that is, it should describe the objects related in some way that is possible.

Exercise 2.3.   This exercise has another ten pairs to try if you believe you need the practice.

seal/finger
bank/doctor
door/hawk
rice/frog
secretary/limousine
beer/airplane
cotton/prince
tack/mustard
cable/chestnut
mayor/tunnel

Now test yourself without looking back at the list.

beer/_____

door/_____

tack/_____

secretary/_____

seal/_____

cable/_____

bank/_____

rice/_____

mayor/_____

cotton/_____

The link mnemonic

The visual imagery used to associate two words can be applied to the problem of remembering a longer list of words, such as a grocery list. Suppose that you want to commit the following shopping list of grocery items to memory: bread, milk, hamburger, a mop, paper napkins, a can of beans, ice cream, pickles, a box of soap, and potato chips. You would like to be able to recall the list as you walk into the grocery store, so make your "cue" for the list the doorway of the grocery store. In order to associate the doorway of the grocery store with your first list item, bread, form a visual image of the door of the grocery store covered with slices of bread. Perhaps the glass door is plastered with slices of bread. To ensure that this image is fixed in your mind, take note of the detail, color, and interaction. Next, think of the two words *bread* and *milk*. Form a visual image of bread and milk interacting in some way. Perhaps, you might think of pieces of bread floating around in a bowl of milk. Again, note detail, color, and interaction. The next word pair on the list is *milk* and *hamburger*. Perhaps you can form a visual image of a carton of milk being poured over a pound of hamburger. The images that have been created so far are diagrammed as shown at the top of the next page.

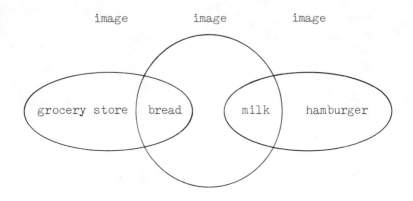

image   image   image

grocery store | bread   milk | hamburger

This diagram shows you why this procedure is called the chain or link mnemonic. Each image is made up of only two words. When the image containing milk and hamburger is made up, you ignore the word *bread*. In this procedure do *not* make up a giant image containing all the words. Make up "links", that is, images containing only two items at a time.

The next pair of words is *hamburger* and *mop*. Perhaps, you might think of a mop handle sticking out of a pound of hamburger. Use any image that occurs to you in which you can see detail, color, and interaction. For *mop* and *paper napkins*, you might think of a mop pushing around a big pile of paper napkins. For *paper napkins* and *can of beans*, what about paper napkins being used to wipe off an overflowing can of beans? For the item *ice cream,* think of a can of beans with a scoop of melting ice cream on top. The next image might be of a container of ice cream being opened and a big dill pickle falling out. Then, a box of soap is poured over the dill pickle in order to clean it off. Finally, the empty soap box is filled with potato chips so that you can have a snack later.

The images formed don't do much for one's appetite, but they will help you to remember that list of grocery items. Check now to see if you can remember the list. Pretend that you are now walking into the grocery store. What do you "see" in the mental picture you have formed? I hope that you can "see" the glass door of the store covered with slices of bread which will be your cue for *loaf of bread*. Next, you should automatically experience a visual image of pieces of bread floating in a bowl of milk, and this should be a cue for the next item *milk*. The chain of images should continue. As image of milk being poured over a pound of hamburger should occur to you next, and so on throughout the list.

*Exercise 2.4.   One problem with the example of grocery store items is that you have used the images that I have described rather than using your own. Here is a list of items that you have to purchase in a hardware store: glue, tacks, some steel wire, a hacksaw, a can of red paint, some copper tubing, lubricating oil, a yardstick, a file, and a small hammer. Start your list with some distinctive feature of your local hardware store, such as the counter, and picture the first item there. Don't forget to use detail, color, and interaction. After forming the images, wait a few minutes, then use the store counter as a starting cue and recall the list. If you have some trouble with this list, check the example solutions at the back of the book where I have described the images I came up with.

Exercise 2.5.   This exercise consists of a list of jobs and errands that Bill Smith has to do today. Can you memorize this list in order? Bill should think of the first item as he gets into his car. The italicized word acts as a cue word for the task, so memorize only the list of cue words.

1. Write *letter* to brother
2. Order *flowers* for wife
3. Pick up *dog* at veterinarian
4. Pick up *airplane* tickets
5. Take *car* to garage
6. Have *oil* changed

7. Have car *tires* checked
8. Mow the *lawn*
9. Buy postage *stamps*
10. Pick up package at *sister's* house
11. Order *opera* tickets
12. Rent *top hat*

If you remember *letter* you will automatically remember *write letter to brother;* if you remember *flowers* you will automatically remember *order flowers for wife.* In Chapter 9 the use of cue words will be discussed more extensively. After you memorize the cue words wait a few minutes and then try to write down the twelve tasks.

*Exercise 2.6.   The link mnemonic not only allows you to remember a list of words, but allows you to remember them in order. Let's say that you are a film enthusiast, and you want to remember the titles of your ten favorite Charlie Chaplin films in the order that they were produced. One such list follows. Try to memorize these titles. As in the previous list, I have tried to make the most easily imaged word in the title the cue word. If you remember the cue word, then you should be able to remember the complete title. Note each image in the link for detail, color, and interaction.

1. Kid *Auto* Races at Venice (first appearance of the "Little Tramp" character)
2. The *Tramp*
3. *Floor* Walker
4. *Pawn Shop*
5. The *Immigrant*
6. Shoulder *Arms*
7. The *Kid*
8. The *Gold* Rush
9. *City* Lights
10. The Great *Dictator* (Chaplin's first "talkie")

When you are finished memorizing, test yourself. If you have trouble with this list, look at the example solutions in the back of the book.

This last list is one that you might want to commit to memory more permanently than the shopping lists or the lists of jobs to do. Once you have finished with those lists there is probably no reason to keep them in memory. Usually they will pretty much disappear from memory after a few days. But what about information you want to remember for a few weeks or months? If you are really interested in the movies, then you may want to remember this list of Chaplin's films permanently. The way to ensure that you will remember this list is to occasionally review the list, with your reviews spaced in time. Test yourself on this list tomorrow. There may be one or two titles that you have trouble remembering. Go through the whole list again recreating the same images while taking note of them for detail, color, and interaction. Concentrate on the images for those items you had trouble remembering. Do the same thing next week. With spaced review you will have committed the list to memory and it will be available for a long time.

The story mnemonic

Another memory technique that is similar to the link mnemonic is the story mnemonic. When using the story mnemonic the words that are to be remembered are made up into a story by adding as many words as needed. Surprisingly, when the story is recalled, there is no problem in discriminating the words from the list from the words you added. Let's try to memorize the following list of twelve words using the story mnemonic: jaw, lawyer, beggar, ram, ship, bill, house, army, scissors, magician, plum, and ski. The story could go something like this:

> John was punched in the *jaw,* so he went to see his *lawyer.* There he met a *beggar* who had a pet *ram.* The ram was on a *ship,* and the beggar could not pay the ram's travel *bill.*

He had already sold his *house* to the *army* and now owned nothing but a pair of magic *scissors*. He used to be a *magician* by trade. As the beggar sat there he ate a *plum* and told John how he loved to *ski*.

When people use the story mnemonic, they usually do not intentionally try to form a series of separate and vivid visual images. However, some visual imagery seems to automatically accompany the events in the story as they are made up, especially when the words to be remembered represent concrete objects. It is probably a good idea to purposely create as many visual images as possible while you create the story.

There seem to be two problems with the story mnemonic. One is that words may be recalled out of order. Words from the list will sometimes fit together very nicely in the story but in an order that is different from their order in the list. When these words are recalled they tend to be recalled not in the list order but in their more natural order. When recalling the above story, you might remember that the beggar used to be a *magician* and owned a pair of magic *scissors*. However, this order of the words is not the order of the words in the list. The second problem in using the story mnemonic is that some words not important to the flow of the story may be left out during recall. In the preceding story the facts that the beggar ate a *plum* and loved to *ski* do not seem relevant to the other events described. In a longer story these less relevant words may be forgotten.

Because of these problems with the story mnemonic I prefer to use the link mnemonic in which the words are dealt with two at a time, and a separate and specific image is formed for each pair of adjacent words. However, you can decide for yourself how frequently you want to use the link mnemonic and the story mnemonic.

*Exercise 2.7. This exercise consists of a list of twelve words: linen, helmet, captain, school, fruit, rocket, cellar, cradle, teacher, needle, beach, and Bible. Create a story using these words. Every time you add a list word to your story try to mentally picture what is happening. When you are finished, wait a few minutes and then try to recall all twelve words in order.

chapter three

Preparing your memory: peg words and loci

In Chapter 1, memory was described as being like a large, floorless closet. Therefore, everything that is to be stored in this closet has to be attached to a peg on the wall. So far, little has been said about what these "pegs" are or how to go about creating them. Chapter 2 dealt with the more basic issue of using visual imagery to associate or link together information. Now, we are ready to concentrate on creating and using these memory pegs. When enough pegs have been created, we will have a way of storing a great deal of information in memory at any one time. However, our skills in using visual imagery will be needed to attach information to these pegs.

The rhyming peg-word mnemonic

First, I would like you to memorize this simple rhyme:

one is a bun, two is a shoe, three is a tree, four is a door,
five is a hive, six are sticks, seven is heaven, eight is a gate,
nine is a line, and ten is a hen.

The word associated with each number rhymes with the number, so the list should be easy to remember. After you have memorized this rhyme, create a visual image for each word in the rhyme. For *one is a bun,* form a visual image of a bun. This can be a hot dog bun, a hamburger bun, a hot cross bun, whatever you wish, as long as it is a clear image. Most often, whatever image you experience first is the image to use. It is important, however, that each time you say to yourself "one is a bun" that you come up with the same image of a bun. The same is true for *two is a shoe.* Form a visual image of a shoe. It can be a gold slipper, a combat boot, whatever. The important thing is that it be a clear image and that you always come up with this same image of a shoe whenever you think of *two is a shoe.* Form all ten images and check each one for detail, color, and interaction just to make sure that they are as clear and vivid as possible.

These ten words are our first set of pegs, and now we are going to use them. Imagine that you are sitting in the dentist's chair anxiously waiting for your dentist to start drilling a tooth. In order to make yourself feel better, you start thinking with pleasure about your family's annual vacation at Lake Tobugee. You begin to reminisce about all the good times and bad times you have experienced there. "For sure," you say to yourself, "I'll remember to bring my insect repellent this year. Also, my tennis racket in case our neighbor challenges us to a game of tennis. I must buy extra batteries for my flashlight." Soon you have thought of a number of items that you must take along this year that you have forgotten in the past. Because you are lying in the dentist's chair with your mouth full of hardware, you cannot get up and write these things down. What you can do, however, is use the rhyming peg-word mnemonic to remember your list in case you want to write it down later. If the first item is *insect repellent,* form a visual image of your first peg word *bun* and insect repellent interacting in some way. You might think of a sandwich made up of your image of a bun with a bottle of insect repellent inside. Check this composite image for detail, color, and interaction. To get interaction, think of the bottle of insect repellent leaking all over the bun. For the next item, tennis racket, form a visual image of a shoe and a tennis racket interacting in some way. You might think of hitting the shoe, your peg word, over the tennis court fence with your tennis racket.

Exercise 3.1. The ten items that you have to remember to take to Lake Tobugee this year are listed. Next to each item I have suggested a visual image. Either use my image or create your own, then be sure to circle *detail, color,* and *interaction* as you "see" each of these in your image.

1. insect repellent—Make a sandwich of a bun and a bottle of insect repellent with the insect repellent leaking on the bun. (detail, color, interaction)

2. tennis racket—A shoe is hit over a fence with a tennis racket. (detail, color, interaction)

3. flashlight batteries—A tree has batteries growing like fruit on it with the wind blowing them down. (detail, color, interaction)

4. playing cards—A door slams on a deck of playing cards and bends them all. (detail, color, interaction)

5. camera—A beehive shaped like a camera has bees flying in and out through the lens. (detail, color, interaction)

6. bathrobe—A bunch of sticks is beating a bathrobe hanging on a hook. (detail, color, interaction)

7. book identifying plants and trees—The angels in heaven are all quietly reading books and turning pages. (detail, color, interaction)

8. rope—A gate is being firmly tied shut with a rope. (detail, color, interaction)
9. pliers—The fishing line being pulled from the water has a large pair of pliers grasping its hook. (detail, color, interaction)
10. knife—A hen is pecking at a knife lying on the ground. (detail, color, interaction)

If you now slowly recite to yourself the ten peg words, each peg word should retrieve from your memory the visual image you formed using that peg word. That image should contain representations of both the peg word and the word that you want to remember. For example, say, "One is a bun." Does a mental image naturally form in your mind? What is in the image? What is the first item in the list that has been associated with bun? Now go through the rest of the peg words and see if you can remember all ten items.

Forming a clear image is the important thing in using the peg-word mnemonic as well as in using all the other mnemonic techniques that will be discussed. The formation of a clear image ensures that the information will be fixed in memory when you are trying to learn it. Always take note of detail, color, and interaction in your images. If you do not adequately store the information in memory to begin with, you will not be able to remember it later.

Exercise 3.2. This exercise has another list of ten items: brush, toast, egg, hand, bow, microscope, shirt, seed, water, and penny. Use the rhyming peg words to memorize this list. Try hard to ignore the items from the list you just learned while you are learning this second list. As you form the image of each peg word, try to blot out or ignore the image of the first list item that may come with it. Create new images that involve only the peg word and the corresponding word from this second list. Next test yourself recalling this list. You should find that the items from the first list, insect repellent, tennis racket, and so on, will *not* be recalled by mistake. You may think of them, but you should quickly be able to decide that they are the wrong set of items. The items of the new list tend to replace the items of previously learned lists of words. This means that you should not reuse the rhyming peg words until you are sure that you are no longer interested in remembering the words that you presently have stored with them.

Exercise 3.3.   This exercise has a third list of ten words: glass, jam, hair, paint, mouse, sofa, plant, nose, net, and rock. Use the rhyming peg-word mnemonic to memorize this list. Try not to think of the words from the first two lists when learning this third list. Make sure you note your visual images for detail, color, and interaction. Test yourself on this third list. You should not experience too much interference from the first two lists you memorized. Moreover, if you try to recall those ten items from the first list that were to be taken to Lake Tobugee this year, you might have some trouble. The list of words most recently attached to the peg words is usually the easiest to recall.

The alphabet peg words

The rhyming peg-word mnemonic is a way of adding ten pegs to memory by which we can store and later recall ten visual images representing information that we wish to memorize. This process of adding pegs to memory will continue with the alphabet peg words. With the alphabet peg words, each letter of the alphabet acts as a memory peg. Although most people find that they can form a visual image of each letter of the alphabet, these visual images do not interact well with the visual images of other things. It is difficult to see detail, color, and interaction in visual images using letters. So what is done in the alphabet mnemonic is to replace each letter with a word that represents some easily pictured concrete object. Furthermore, the letter is replaced by a word that sounds somewhat like the letter, so that the word can be more easily remembered.

Exercise 3.4. Following are listed words which sound somewhat like each of the letters of alphabet. Go through the list and circle one word to represent each letter. Choose a peg word that you can easily visualize that sounds to you somewhat like the letter it is supposed to represent. The first word next to each letter is my choice, and will be the peg word that I will use in the examples.

A—ape, hay, ace, ale
B—beet, bee, bead, bean, beer, beef, beach
C—seal, seat, seed, sea, seer
D—dean, deal, deep, deer, deed
E—eel, ear
F—frog, fowl, fire, fly, face, fox, fan
G—jeans, jeep, giant, gin, giraffe, gym, gypsy
H—hat, hail, hoe, ham
I—ice, eye, isle
J—blue jay, jail, jade
K—cane, case, cave, cone, cake, cage
L—elk, elf, elm
M—emperor, emblem, hem, emcee, emerald, ember
N—engine, end, hen
O—ogre, oaf, oak, oar, oats
P—pea, peak, peel, piece
Q—cue, cube, cure
R—arm, arc, art, ark, hour
S—eskimo, escort, ass
T—tee, tea, team, teen, tears
U—U-boat, ukulele, eunuch, Europe
V—Venus, veal, VIP
W—double goo, double ooze, double view
X—ax, ox, X-ray, exit

Y—wine, wife, wiper, wire
Z—zebra, zero

If some word occurs to you that works well but is not on the list, then use it. Note that the words chosen sound like the letter each is paired with, but often the word does not start with that letter. This is true for the word *sea* representing the letter C. There is a good reason for this. When you use the alphabet peg words you will probably be saying the letters to yourself rather than writing the letters down on paper. So a word that will be remembered as representing a letter is one that should sound like that letter rather than look like it. If you wish to, you can make up peg words that always begin with the letter each word represents. But remember that (1) the word must be reliably recalled from the letter, and (2) the word must be easily visualized.

Exercise 3.5. Once you have chosen a peg word to represent each of the twenty-six letters, study those words until you can recall them easily.

Exercise 3.6. After you have memorized the alphabet peg words you can use them in exactly the same way as the rhyming peg words. Here is a list of twenty-six words: cannon, quarter, crown, bouquet, saucer, hatchet, spear, globe, broom, cord, film, pickle, trumpet, pants, fence, magazine, alcohol, ant, kettle, wire, couch, bandage, tangerine, beetle, stomach, and wheel. Use visual imagery to associate each of these words with the respective alphabet peg word. Make sure you take note of the detail, color, and interaction in each image. To ensure that you have successfully associated the peg words and the words from the list, review all twenty-six interacting images after you have formed them. Next go through the alphabet, generate the alphabet peg words, and write down words from the list by "decoding" the images that you experience.

Exercise 3.7. This exercise has another list of twenty-six words to test yourself with using the alphabet peg words: pan, soda, teeth, chicken, goat, map, butter, soil, crocodile, plate, artist, soot, silver, sun, flannel, mother, cucumber, hospital, sleigh, tank, concrete, ocean, icicle, telephone, brother, and baby.

The method of loci

In ancient Greece and Rome, students of rhetoric used a peg-type mnemonic called the method of loci (the method of places). What they would do is memorize a series of locations from some place such as a public building and then use the visual images of those locations as pegs or hooks to which they would attach important words and ideas from a speech they were to give. When it came time to give this speech, the orator would mentally go through the loci one by one and pick out the next important word or idea in his speech as each was needed. In this way a well-organized and often long speech could be given without the use of notes.

This method is very similar to the peg-word techniques that we have previously discussed, except that visual images of places are used as pegs rather than visual images of things. To get a better feel for the method of loci it might be good to go through an example. Let's say that you wanted to make up a list of ten loci to use as pegs. You could use ten locations from your house or apartment. First choose a starting point, perhaps you could think of getting up in the morning. That sounds like a reasonable place to start. As you try to think up loci, make sure that you can form a clear and vivid visual image of a place before you decide to use it. Also, try not to make your loci too similar to one another. The first location could be the foot of your bed. The second locus could be your night table. If you don't have a night table, choose some other object or piece of furniture in your bedroom. The third location is an open dresser drawer. Next, walk into the bathroom. The fourth location is the toilet, the fifth the bathtub, and the sixth the sink. Try to make the order of the loci follow the order that you would encounter them in your morning routine. If the order of locations I have suggested here is not appropriate for you, change them around. The seventh location could be the medicine cabinet. Now walk into the kitchen. The eighth location is the inside of the refrigerator, the ninth the cupboard, and the tenth the top of the stove. Certainly, additional loci could be chosen, but these will do for now.

To review, our ten locations are:

1. the foot of the bed
2. the night table
3. an open dresser drawer
4. the toilet
5. the bathtub
6. the sink
7. the medicine cabinet
8. the inside of the refrigerator
9. the cupboard
10. the top of the stove

To memorize a list of items, the loci are used in the same way as peg words. Let's say that you have to remember to bring the following ten items to a party, and when you were told to do so, you didn't have a pencil or a pen so you couldn't write them down. Here is the list: brandy, an accordion, coffee, marshmallows, cigars, candles, lemons, aspirin, mints, and a bagpipe. As in all peg-type mnemonics, interacting images must be formed between each locus and the corresponding item to be remembered. Make sure that you note each image for detail, color, and interaction. For the first item, form a visual image of a bottle of brandy lying at the foot of your bed. What does the label look like? What color is the bottle? In your imagination see the bottle rolling around on your bed. Next, form a visual image of an accordion on your night table. Maybe it has knocked the clock onto the floor. As you open your dresser drawer you see a can of coffee. Some has spilled on your socks. In the toilet marshmallows are floating around. Flush them! In the bathtub is a box of smoking cigars. Turn the water on them. Now where are you? At the sink, right? In the sink are some birthday candles. Rinse them down the drain. When you open the medicine cabinet, a lemon falls out. When you finally get to the kitchen, you open up the refrigerator and see a giant bottle of aspirin. The cupboard is filled with chocolate mints. A bagpipe sitting on top of the stove is getting scorched.

Did you take note of the detail, color, and interaction for each image formed? Good. Now, what were those items? Go through the locations and recall the list of items you have to take to the party. Be careful. With the method of loci it's easy to miss an item. There is no system of reliably going from one locus to the next as in the rhyming peg-word mnemonic or in the alphabetic mnemonic. You would not be likely to leave out a number or letter when you use those systems. But if you mentally *walk too fast* and mentally *don't keep your eyes open*, then you might miss a locus and thereby forget an item.

The walk-through-life loci

One problem with the previous example is that I chose loci with which I was familiar, but perhaps you were not. You may not have a medicine cabinet. You may have a shower but no bathtub. So now it is time for you to make up some locations of use in memorizing. In fact, you are going to make up 100 of them. With 100 loci, you will be able to memorize a list of 100 items. But if you have 100 of anything (books, phonograph records, indoor plants, shirts), then you have to organize them in some way to find the one you want later. With 100 loci it could be difficult for you to reliably recall the loci in their correct order and keep track of where you are in the list when you use them. In order to overcome these two problems, the loci will be organized into subparts.

One hundred locations that are easily imaged, easily recalled, and fairly distinct from one another is a large order to fill. So what I am going to ask you to do is to draw on all your life experiences in order to come up with these 100 loci. First, the 100 loci should be made up from ten general locations. The general locations early in the list should be drawn from those places you experienced early in your life but which you can still visualize. These general locations might include your parents' house (upstairs), your parents' house (downstairs), your parents' yard, their garage, your neighborhood, your grandparents' house, or some other close relative's house. The only requirement is that these general locations be familiar to you. Some other general locations might include a church, your grade school, a place where your family often vacationed, a favorite park or playground, and a camp you used to attend. These general locations will provide specific loci.

Next move to your high-school years. General locations of loci might include specific places in your high-school building, the high-school hangout, the place where you had a part-time job. Continue choosing general locations or places from college or from the various jobs you had and places you lived or visited. The only requirement is that you are familiar enough with the general location so that you will be able to generate five to ten specific locations from each general one. If a general location yields only five distinct loci, then two related general locations can be used to come up with the necessary ten loci.

So, the ten general categories might be:

1. Parents' house
2. Parents' yard and garage
3. Grandparents' house
4. Church

5. Grade school
6. High school and high-school hangout
7. Job at supermarket
8. Vacation spot
9. College dormitory
10. College campus

Of course, I have created this list only because we need an example to work with. *You* create your own group of ten general locations using *your* life experiences.

Exercise 3.8. Create a list of ten general locations. Arrange the ten general locations so that if you looked at a map of these locations you could go from one to another in a simple manner without a lot of zigzagging and crisscrossing. In the example list that I have given I can imagine myself walking, driving, or flying from my parents' house to my grandparents' house, then to the church, then to the grade school, then to the high school, then to the supermarket, and so on. If these locations were arranged differently, then I would change their order to keep my "walk" as simple as possible.

The next step is to take each general location and from it create two sets of five specific locations. As with the general locations, the simple locations should be sequenced so that you can mentally "see" each in turn as you "walk" from one to the other. If you have trouble getting ten loci from one general location, two related general locations may be put together as was done for general location number 6 above: high school and high-school hangout. Here is an example of how two sets of five specific locations can be created from one general location:

1. Parents' house
   kitchen: refrigerator, stove (top), stove (oven), sink, cupboard
   living room: sofa, TV, bookcase, chair, lamp

Note that you may be able to get more loci out of a large, familiar location like your parents' house than has been done here. However, make sure that all the loci are relatively distinct from one another. For example, don't use four identical living room chairs as four different loci. Their images may be so much alike that each one will not act as a distinct cue, and you won't be able to remember the four different items placed on the four chairs. If you are going to use more than one chair or table in a particular room, then make sure that you use very different looking pieces of furniture. One chair may be large, red, and well-padded. The other could be small, brown, and made of polished wood. Image them this way to make them distinct.

Let's continue with another example list of specific loci:

2. Parents' yard and garage
   yard: wooden fence, gate, big tree, sandbox, swing
   garage: roof, big door, inside shelf, hooks on wall, lawn mower
3. Grandparents' house
   bathroom: shower stall, toilet, sink, medicine cabinet, shelf
   dining room: bureau, counter, chandelier, table, chair
4. Church
   chapel: pew, pulpit, communion rail, choir, window
   meeting room: podium, chair, table, flag, piano
5. Grade school
   playground: slide, swing, climbing bars, large tire, steps
   classroom: teacher, teacher's desk, fishbowl, blackboard, my desk
6. High school and high-school hangout
   hall: outside steps, front door, trophy case, water fountain, school banner
   hangout: coat rack, stool, counter, jukebox, shelf of glasses
7. Job at supermarket
   front: grocery carts, cashier, cash register, office door, stack of paper bags
   back: shelf of beer bottles, shelf of apples, freezer of ice cream, cooler of meat, shelf of canned soup

8. Vacation spot
   dock: canoe, paddle, beach, towel, fishing pole
   tent: tent pole, cot, knapsack, tent rope, campfire
9. College dormitory
   room: closet, desk, chair, bed, lamp
   dining hall: ticket taker, tray, counter with food, dining table, window
10. College campus
    outside library: steps, sculpture, president's house, fence, bridge
    inside library: gate, elevator, card catalogue, book return, window

In the examples of loci given here few were taken from any one place. You might be able to form two or even three sets of ten loci from where you went to school or from where you have worked. Many people prefer to use loci that all appear in the same general location. Some people can easily create 100 loci using only locations in their houses. Also, in the example used here loci such as *table, chair,* and *window* occur more than once but in different places. This should cause no problems as long as the images of the various tables, chairs, and windows are different and occur in different contexts.

Exercise 3.9. Make up your own list of 100 Walk-Through-Life Loci. Use the ten general locations you created in Exercise 3.8 and from each general location create two sets of five loci each. You may have to do some adjusting of your ten general locations to get things to work out right. Arrange the 100 loci so that they follow a natural sequence. Also, within each set arrange the loci in the same order that they would occur as you walked past the various locations. This will make them easier to remember in the correct order.

Exercise 3.10. Study the 100 loci until you can recall them in order. Also, make sure that you are aware of the transition from one general location to another and the transition from one set of five to another. This will help you keep track of where you are in the list.

Exercise 3.11. After not having looked at your loci for at least a day, try to recall all 100 in order. If you cannot, then review them.

Exercise 3.12. Use your loci to memorize the following list of 100 items (in order). Because the list is long, go through the list twice before you test yourself. Make sure that you form the same locus/item composite image each time. Check each image for detail, color, and interaction. With a list of words this long, the problem may arise of having a word on the list be the same as one of your loci. The 100th list word is *table,* and a type of table may occur one or more times as one of your loci. Make sure that when you form a visual image of the list word *table* it is very different from the image you use for any of your loci that are tables. There is a good reason for this. If you create two different composite images and each one has exactly the same table in it that represents one of your loci, you may later experience difficulty in remembering. When using the locus that is a table as a cue, you may recall both images or the wrong one. To minimize this problem make the image for the list word *table* distinct from the locus *table* in any way you can. Mentally paint a big, red *X* on it. At recall the red *X* will indicate to you that the table is a list word and not one of your loci.

1.	chopstick	10.	banana	19.	hook	28.	rope
2.	soldier	11.	stool	20.	dresser	29.	whistle
3.	bucket	12.	gown	21.	plow	30.	doughnut
4.	tiger	13.	pajamas	22.	telescope	31.	frog
5.	leg	14.	wallet	23.	ticket	32.	soup
6.	purse	15.	nest	24.	potato	33.	flute
7.	pear	16.	zipper	25.	cent	34.	necklace
8.	mosquito	17.	baton	26.	gravel	35.	noodles
9.	pot	18.	lard	27.	sword	36.	whip

37. whiskey	53. ice cream	69. umbrella	85. bubble
38. ape	54. eagle	70. toothpaste	86. clover
39. cardinal	55. quilt	71. magnet	87. princess
40. jet	56. bowl	72. bed	88. ring
41. cottage	57. balloon	73. yacht	89. tray
42. tulip	58. fish	74. steak	90. bolt
43. mast	59. phone	75. cake	91. oatmeal
44. vase	60. rug	76. trolley	92. glove
45. trailer	61. rifle	77. engine	93. wax
46. toe	62. train	78. stick	94. lamp
47. duck	63. book	79. acrobat	95. peach
48. jello	64. skull	80. candy	96. ink
49. lamb	65. macaroni	81. toy	97. rock
50. car	66. sponge	82. spinach	98. deer
51. handlebars	67. timepiece	83. salt	99. shawl
52. strawberry	68. pedal	84. fork	100. table

Now test yourself by writing down all 100 words in order from memory.

chapter four

Substitution techniques for remembering abstract words

Can you guess the answers to the following riddles?

1. In what country is the use of pencils prohibited?
2. In what country is scuba diving the national sport?
3. What country is known for its mechanical cows?
4. What country has the strangest shape?
5. What country has the unhealthiest climate?
6. What countries are known for their slippery streets?
7. What country has too many dogs?
8. What country has the most restaurants?
9. What country has the largest number of barber shops?
10. What country has the largest houses?

11. In what country does everyone wear shorts?
12. In what country do they celebrate Thanksgiving three times a year?

Answers: 1. Ink-land, 2. Fin-land, 3. Bull-gear-ia, 4. Cube-a, 5. Germ-many, 6. Grease, Ice-land, and You-go-slide-ia, 7. Howl-land 8. Hungry, 9. Pole-land, 10. Room-mania, 11. Thigh-land, 12. Turkey.

I apologize for the awful puns. But punning, which includes the use of a word as some other word that it sounds like, is an important technique for remembering and will be discussed extensively in this chapter. I hope that those of you who can't stand puns will bear (Grrrr) with me.

If a situation arises in which words have to be memorized such as *Romania, Thailand,* and *Yugoslavia,* or even words such as *concept, method,* or *information,* the techniques that have been discussed in previous chapters do not work well, because for most people these words do not represent familiar, physical objects that can be easily imaged. There are a number of ways around this problem that will be discussed, but first let's look at a list of words that are fairly difficult to memorize. These ten words represent ten important principles of memorization, and it would be good for us as students of mnemonic techniques to be able to recall and dwell upon these ten principles whenever we have the opportunity. Here they are:

1. *Interest*—To better remember information we should be interested in it. Schoolboys who perform poorly in the classroom can often remember a great deal of information about their favorite baseball players.

2. *Attention*—No matter how intrinsically interesting information is, you must attend to it if it is to be remembered. This means thinking about it.

3. *Meaningfulness*—The more meaningful the information, the better it will be remembered. For example, if you take the words of a simple sentence and mix them up, the words will be harder to remember. It

is easy to remember the list of words, *The girl ate the cake.* It is more difficult to remember the list, *cake the ate girl the.*

4. *Organization*—If a person is asked to recall as many of the fifty states as possible, a good way to recall them is to first think of the individual states in one geographic region; that is, recall all of the states in New England, then all of the states in the East, then all the states in the South, and so on. Recalling the states as they come to mind without taking advantage of their geographic organization results in poorer recall performance.

5. *Association*—Is there a way to remember that Romania is just north of Bulgaria? If the word *room* is associated with Romania and the word *bull* is associated with Bulgaria, then the image can be formed of a bull carrying a small room on its back, where *on top of* means *to the north of.*

6. *Visualization*—Effective association of words often takes place by forming visual images made up of those things the words represent.

7. *Repetition*—With very long lists of words you may have to go through the list more than once and review your images in order to later remember the list correctly.

8. *Feedback*—Test yourself. If you find that you cannot remember as well as you should when using some mnemonic technique, then you are doing something wrong.

9. *Review*—Some lists of words such as peg words or loci you may want to remember longer than a day or two. You should therefore occasionally review these lists to make sure that you don't forget them.

10. *Spacing*—If information must be repeatedly studied because of its length or reviewed because you want to remember it permanently, then spacing the study of the material in time will result in better retention. Spacing your study over time is better than studying and restudying the material all in one sitting.

Use of sentences

How can this list of ten words be committed to memory? Because there are ten words, the rhyming peg-word mnemonic might be a way to do it, but how can visual images be formed? Using the rhyming peg-word mnemonic, the first peg is *one is a bun,* and the first list word is *interest.* How can a bun and an *interest* be visualized as interacting? Most people have trouble forming a visual image of an *interest*. For the moment let's forget about forming visual images. Rather, let's try to deal with the list in a purely verbal way. You may remember that in Chapter 2 some suggestions were given for people who have trouble forming visual images. Now may be the time for all of us to try to make use of those suggestions. The idea here is to make up sentences with as much imagery in them as possible, even though the words that we want to remember may not be part of the image. Let's not forget to take note of detail, color, and interaction whenever possible.

1. Interest—This bun has on it a design of great *interest*.
2. Attention—My shoes of gold attracted a great deal of *attention*.
3. Meaningfulness—The tree has a message carved on it of great *meaningfulness*.
4. Organization—That door leads to the office of a powerful *organization*.
5. Association—A hive is where bees are in *association*.
6. Visualization—A stick hit him and he experienced the *visualization* of stars.
7. Repetition—You can get to heaven by *repetition* of your prayers.
8. Feedback—The gate will stay open and not *feedback*.
9. Review—His fishing line pulled up a *review* of his book.
10. Spacing—The hens roosted with even *spacing*.

Now use the rhyming peg words to determine if you can recall the ten words. This technique works moderately well for most people, but many memory experts believe that because the words that are to be remembered are not really part of a visual image, they will be easily forgotten. Consequently, we will use the sentence technique only as a back-up technique when it is difficult to find high-imagery substitutes for the words. If the use of sentences works very well for you and better than the substitution techniques that we are going to talk about, then use it often. Remember, though, that many of these mnemonic techniques require a fair amount of practice before you become proficient with them. Don't give up and go back to using a less efficient mnemonic, such as the sentence mnemonic, simply because at first it is easier to use.

Use of high-imagery semantic substitutions

Another possible way of dealing with these abstract words is to replace them with associated words that can be easily visualized. By remembering these associated words through the use of visual images, the original words will be remembered. Let's create some high-imagery words that are associated with the ten words from the preceding list.

1. Interest—a building that is a savings bank
2. Attention—a soldier standing up at attention
3. Meaningfulness—somebody winking his or her eye at you
4. Organization—an automobile assembly line
5. Association—a group of people having a meeting
6. Visualization—a television set
7. Repetition—a printing press printing the same page over and over
8. Feedback—a report card
9. Review—a Broadway review
10. Spacing—a spaceship in outer space

The next thing to do is to connect these images with one another using the link mnemonic or connect them to one of our set of pegs. Let's use the first ten pegs of the alphabetic mnemonic.

1. ape + interest—An ape is climbing up the front of a bank.
2. beet + attention—A beet is on the rifle of the soldier standing at attention.
3. seal + meaningfulness—A person riding a seal is winking an eye at you.
4. dean + organization—A college dean in his academic robe is working on an assembly line.

5. eel + association—A group of eels are having a meeting.
6. frog + visualization—A person is watching a frog in a television show.
7. jeans + repetition—Everyone is in jeans working at the printing press.
8. hat + feedback—A little kid in a big hat is looking at his report card.
9. ice + review—a large ice skating arena is used to stage a Broadway review.
10. blue jay + spacing—a blue jay is captain of a spaceship in outer space.

Now go back and recall the alphabet peg words and the associated images. Can you recall the abstract words from the images that have been stored in memory? You have already had a fair amount of practice with this list, but recall of the words may still be difficult. Words like *organization* and *association* are close enough in meaning that they are sometimes confused with one another. Also, the image may be clearly remembered, but the abstract word the image is supposed to represent can be lost. I had a difficult time getting the word *repetition* out of the image of a printing press. Well, let's try something else.

Use of high-imagery phonetic substitutions

Some words have meanings that are related, such as *interest* and *bank*, and some words have pronunications that are related, such as *England* and *Ink-land*. Yes, we have returned to the subject of punning and will now attempt to find a concrete word or string of words to substitute for an abstract word that cannot be imaged. These phonetic substitutions do not have to sound exactly like the original pronunciations of the words. In fact, you will see below some substitutions that are quite different in sound from the original words. However, as long as there is some similarity in sound between the first substitute word and the first one or two syllables of the original word, then the substitute word can be an effective cue for the word that you want to remember.

What about the word *interest*? Finding one substitute word

or a string of short substitute words for *interest* is not easy. First, make sure that your substitute words pronounced together sound something like the abstract word you are replacing. Second, make sure that your substitute words represent concrete objects for which visual images can be formed. Third, decide whether you want to represent the entire word phonetically or just the first one or two syllables. This decision is sometimes a difficult one. You could encode *interest* as *intern* using the first two syllables, or as *intern:nest* using all three syllables. You have to decide whether you will be able to later remember the word *interest* with only the cue *intern* available to you. If not, you may have to code *interest* using both the substitute words *intern* and *nest*. *Intern* and *nest* also can be associated using the link mnemonic (Chapter 2). Perhaps you could visualize a young intern (a medical doctor in training) as sitting in a large bird's nest. Later, when you remember *intern* you will also remember *nest* because of your visual image, and these two substitute words will provide you with enough phonetic cues to remember the original word *interest*.

Only with experience will you be able to decide whether you should code *interest* simply as *intern* or as *intern:nest*. As an inexperienced mnemonist, you do not know now how many phonetic cues it takes for you to remember an abstract word. I will usually use only one or two in the examples and place additional ones in parentheses.

What if you can't easily visualize an intern? Then you shouldn't use the word intern as a substitute word. Use some other words. Perhaps *ant:ear:(nest)*. What about *hint:her:(nest)*? Although *hint* and *her* meet our first requirement of phonetic similarity to the original word, *hint* and *her* are not easily imageable and therefore do not meet our second requirement. *Hint* does not represent a specific concrete object, nor does *her*.

The following list consists of ten words from our original list with corresponding phonetic substitutes. You may come up with others that are better. Just make sure that the substitute words are concrete and easily visualized. One other point: Don't get discouraged. Doing this for the first time is difficult for most people, and the word *interest* is a difficult word with which to start. However, if you persevere, the task becomes easier. You will learn some substitutions that can be used often. For example, the syllable *ing* can be coded as *ink*, the syllable *i* can be made into *eye*, and the syllable *or* into *oar*. The substitute words in parentheses should be used in addition to the other substitute words only if you think that you need them as cues in order to remember the original word.

1. Interest—*ant:ear:(nest)*
2. Attention—*ad:tent:(shin)*
3. Meaningfulness—*man:ink:(fool:nose)*
4. Organization—*organ:eye:(station)*
5. Association—*ass:oats:(apron)*
6. Visualization—*fish:zoo:(alley:acorn)*
7. Repetition—*ray:petition*
8. Feedback—*feet:back (or feed:bag)*
9. Review—*reef:goo*
10. Spacing—*spice:ink*

The next task is to connect each of the sequences of words with a peg word. Let's use the next ten peg words in the alphabet mnemonic, representing the letters K to T. Listed below are my peg words, all my substitute words and my images. You can read through these carefully to get an idea of the procedure, or, if you feel more confident, use your own peg words, substitute words, and images whenever you can. Because most of abstract words have been replaced by more than one substitute word, use the link mnemonic to connect the peg word with the first of the substitute words, then the first substitute word with the second substitute word, and so on. Note each image in the chain for detail, color, and interaction.

1. cane—*ant:ear:(nest)*—A cane hits an ant. The ant falls on his ear. (His ear swells up to look like a bird's nest.)

2. elk—*ad:tent:(shin)*—An elk is trying to eat an advertisement for food. The ad is about a tent. (Sticking out of the tent is someone's shin.)

3. emperor—*man:ink:(fool:nose)*—An emperor is standing on a man. The man is covered with ink. (The ink is being washed off by a fool. The fool has a large nose.)

4. engine—*organ:eye:(station)*—A gasoline engine powers an organ. The organ has an eye painted on it. (The organ is in the police station.)

5. ogre—*ass:oats:(apron)*—An ogre is petting his ass. The ass is eating oats. (The oats are in the pockets of an apron.)

6. pea—*fish:zoo:(alley:acorn)*—A pea shot from a pea shooter hits a fish. The fish is in the zoo. (The zoo is in an alley. The alley is covered with acorns.)

7. cue—*ray:petition*—A pool cue shoots out a deadly ray. The ray incinerates a petition to the governor.

8. arm—*feet:back*—I use my arm to scratch my feet. I use my feet to scratch my back.

9. eskimo—*reef:goo*—An eskimo is caught on a coral reef. The reef is covered with a slimy goo.

10. tee—*spice:ink*—Instead of a golf ball the tee has a bottle of spice on it. Suddenly ink begins to run out of the bottle.

Now go through these ten peg words and try to recall the words. The first letter used for this list was K.

Not too hard, was it? The difficult problem in using phonetic substitution procedures is coming up with concrete words that can be visualized. Actually remembering these concrete substitute words is not the most difficult step and is something that you have practiced doing in previous chapters. Another point to keep in mind is that even if you do not remember all the substitute words used for an abstract word, recalling the first substitute word may be enough of a hint to allow you to recall the original word.

The following exercises all deal with the method of phonetic substitution. In the long run it is probably the most effective word substitution procedure, but, unfortunately, it is the one that requires the most practice to use efficiently.

*Exercise 4.1.   Phonetically encode the following list of abstract words. Substitute one concrete word for one or two syllables at a time. Also, you may need to use substitute words for only the first one or two syllables of each word. The number of syllables of each word you encode depends on the number of substitute words you think you will need to recall the original word. Some of the words represent people's last names. Using substitution techniques on proper nouns will become important in later chapters.

1.	panorama	8.	role	15.	owner	22.	pollution
2.	tradition	9.	commercial	16.	wrath	23.	Applebaum
3.	Collier	10.	Weintraub	17.	Lawrence	24.	labor
4.	mutiny	11.	ambition	18.	shriek	25.	victory
5.	danger	12.	social	19.	donor	26.	cowardice
6.	Flanagan	13.	Tuttle	20.	Washington		
7.	mortgage	14.	stare	21.	verb		

*Exercise 4.2.   This exercise has a list of ten abstract words. For each abstract word do the following: (1) Create one or more substitute concrete words for each abstract word. (2) Use the rhyming peg-word mnemonic to memorize the ten sets of substitute words. (3) If there is more than one substitute word for any abstract word, use the link mnemonic to connect the peg word with the first substitute word, the first substitute word with the second substitute word, and so on until the sequence of words is linked together. (4) Note each visual image for detail, color, and interaction. (5) After you have used the mnemonic, write down the numbers one to ten and recall the ten abstract words. Do this by generating each peg word. From the peg word generate the sequence of images connected to that peg word. Next, write down the substitute words. Repeat the

string of substitute words so that it acts as a cue for the sound of the abstract word. Finally, write down the abstract word.

1. term
2. knowledge
3. ceremony
4. Knapp
5. device
6. retreat
7. Bradley
8. despair
9. democracy
10. meeting

Exercise 4.3. Go back to the twenty-six words in Exercise 4.1 and use the alphabet mnemonic to memorize the twenty-six sets of substitute words you generated in Exercise 4.1. Go through the list twice and form the same set of images each time. In this case it is important to go through the list twice. The list is long, and some abstract words have more than one substitute word replacing them. Use the same procedure as outlined in Exercise 4.2. Test yourself by writing the letters a to z on a sheet of paper and recalling the abstract word that goes with each letter.

chapter five

Remembering numbers

Numbers, like abstract words, are difficult to remember. The problem with abstract words is that they cannot be easily imaged. The problem with numbers is somewhat different. Numbers such as 27 and 92 can be pictured mentally. However, these numbers are not meaningful to most people, unless one of them happens to represent your age, house or apartment number, or something like that. Even if you form visual images of numbers, it is sometimes difficult to get them to *interact* with the images of other things. Their images do not easily show detail, color, or interaction. These are the same problems that occur when forming visual images of letters.

In this chapter numbers will be memorized by first transforming them using a substitution technique that was developed especially for numbers. Using this procedure each digit in a number is transformed into a letter that is a consonant. After this is done for each digit in a number, any number of vowels (a, e, i, o, u) are added to the consonants so that one or more words are formed. In this system vowels do not represent any digits, nor do the letters w, h, or y. With this sytem, instead of trying to remember numbers, you try to remember concrete words, which is a much easier task. Later, these words are transformed back into the original numbers. In this digit-consonant mnemonic the first thing we have to look at is what consonants can be substituted for each digit.

digit	consonant sound	hint to help remember
0	z, s, or soft c	the first sound of zero is z
1	t or d	t or d has a vertical line in it when printed
2	n	n has two vertical lines in it when printed
3	m	m has three vertical lines in it when printed
4	r	four ends in r
5	l	four fingers straight up with thumb out form the letter l l is the Roman letter for 50
6	ch, j, sh, or soft g	a 6 looks like a backward j
7	k, hard c, hard g, or qu	a capital k can be made out of two 7s
8	f, v, or ph	an eight and a handwritten f look similar
9	p or b	9 and p are mirror images

The consonant sounds that can be substituted for a given digit are pronounced somewhat similarly, and any one of them can be used. If you want to be able to remember at least one sound for each of the digits 0, 1, 2, 3, 4, 5, 6, 7, 8, and 9, try to remember the sentence *Satan may relish coffee pie.* *Satan* represents 012 because when the vowels are removed the consonant sounds *s, t,* and *n* remain. *May* represents 3 because of the consonant sound *m.* *Relish* represents 456 because of the sounds *r, l,* and *sh. Coffee* represents 78 because of the sounds *hard c* or *k* and *f.* Finally, *pie* represents 9 because of the sound *p.* All the sounds are consonant sounds. The sounds for the vowels a, e, i, o, and u have no numerical values. Neither do the letters w, h, and y. These letters are added to the consonants so that concrete words can be formed. When you later recall the words, these vowels and the letters w, h, and y are ignored, and only the consonant sounds are translated back into digits. Concentrate on the sound of the words, not on the spelling. Often you will be using these techniques without the use of pencil and paper. It is easier to say the sound of a word to yourself than to try to visualize its spelling.

Consider the word *soccer.* The consonant sounds are *s, k,* and *r,* so this word represents the number 074. The vowels o and e are ignored. The two c's are pronounced as k. The word *scallops* represents 07590. *Exit* is 701 because the consonant sounds are *k, s,* and *t.*

*Exercise 5.1.   Translate the following words into digits using the digit-consonant mnemonic.

1. jello
2. sea
3. thunder
4. tennis
5. hall
6. church
7. mahogany
8. night
9. lamb
10. gift

11. boulder	16. shrug
12. knife	17. vault
13. colonel	18. garage
14. biscuit	19. sidewalk
15. bouquet	20. surf

*Exercise 5.2. Transform the following numbers into words representing concrete objects that can be easily imaged. As a first step, print the possible consonant sounds below each digit. Next, add the filler letters *a, e, i, o,* and *u* and *w, h,* and *y* until you come up with a concrete word or a pair of words. Example:

$$
\begin{array}{rcc}
\text{Numbers:} & 1 & 5 \\
\text{Possible consonant sounds:} & t & 1 \\
& d & - \\
\end{array}
$$

Filler letters added: *too*l, *to*ll, *do*ll, *do*ll*y*, *di*al, *t*a*l*l*ow*

1. 8	11. 62
2. 0	12. 2
3. 37	13. 007
4. 66	14. 5
5. 1	15. 9
6. 309	16. 083
7. 11	17. 4
8. 3	18. 94
9. 691	19. 277
10. 6	20. 7

The 100 peg-word mnemonic

The digit-consonant mnemonic is very useful for creating long lists of peg words. We are now going to create another list of 100 peg words to add to the 10 rhyming peg words, the 26 alphabetic peg words, and the 100 Walk-Through-Life loci that you have already memorized. You may feel that the walls of your memory closet are filled to capacity with pegs. This is not true. There is still plenty of room. For example, if you want to add another set of 26 peg words based on the shapes of the letters of the alphabet rather than on their sounds, you will find that you have little trouble adding 26 more. For the alphabet peg words based on shape choose a peg word for the letter *A* that looks like the capital letter *A*. You might choose *tent,* because a capital *A* looks like the front of a tent. The peg word for capital letter *B* could be *spectacles,* because *B* looks like a pair of spectacles standing on their side. The total of 236 peg words that you are asked to memorize in this book is only a good beginning.

Exercise 5.3.   Now let's go about generating this new set of 100 peg words based on the digit-consonant mnemonic. (1) Write down the numbers 1 to 100 on a sheet of paper. (2) Look at the Appendix in the back of this book. Next to each of the numbers 1 to 100 is a list of words. Using the rules of the digit-consonant mnemonic, each of the words in each set is equivalent to the number next to it. (3) Carefully read each word in each set and try to form a visual image of the *object* the word represents. For example, when you read the word *tie* for number 1, try to visual a bow tie or a regular tie that is worn. Don't try to visualize a baseball game with a tie score. If you are not sure of the meaning of a word, look it up in the dictionary. (4) Choose the word from each set that you get the clearest visual image for. This will be your peg word for that number. Also, try to choose peg words that are different from the words you chose for the alphabet mnemonic and for the 100 loci. If you do use a word again, try to make up and use an image that is very distinct from the image used in the other set. Once you choose a peg word, you should always form exactly the same image for that peg word. The first word in each list is the word that I will be using in my examples.

The 100 peg-word mnemonic will be used in the same way as the other peg words and loci that you have memorized. It's useful to have all these peg words because you can simultaneously keep in memory two 100 item lists using the 100 loci for one list and the 100 peg words for the other. Because the peg words and loci are distinct, the 2 sets of items will not become confused with one another. The 100 peg words can be broken into parts somewhat more easily than can the 100 loci. For example, if you had to remember 5 lists of 20 items each, you could use pegs 1 to 20 for the first list, 21 to 40 for the second, and so on. It may be easier finding your way around the 100 peg words than it is finding your way around the 100 loci.

In addition, the 100 peg words will provide a ready-made set of words that you can substitute for one- and two-digit numbers. This will be a great convenience when using some later mnemonics involving historic dates, prices, telephone numbers, and other kinds of numeric information.

Even though the 100 peg words follow the digit-consonant substitution rules, some effort must be made to memorize them. Whenever you think of a number from 1 to 100, the corresponding peg word should instantly come to mind. What are the peg words for 27, or 84, or 43? Does it take more than a few seconds to remember each one? Don't get discouraged. The following series of exercises will help you commit the 100 peg words to memory.

Exercise 5.4. Think of the 100 peg words as 10 sets of 10 words each. Take the first set of 10. Use the link mnemonic to connect peg word number 1 to peg word number 2. Then connect peg word number 2 to peg word number 3. Continue in this way until you have connected together the first 10 peg words. Now try to recall all 10. If you can do this, go on to the second set of 10 and use the link mnemonic to memorize those. Your cue for the second set will be the number 11, so you do have to know what the peg word is for 11. Memorize each of the 10 sets separately in this way. Now, write down the numbers 1 to 100. Using *both* the digit-consonant mnemonic for the numbers 1, 11, 21, 31, and so on, and your 10 chains of visual images, write down all 100 peg words.

Exercise 5.5.   If you have successfully completed Exercise 5.4, you are now ready to take another step toward complete memorization of the 100 peg words. Use 100 index cards or 100 slips of paper, and on one side of each card print a peg word and on the other side print the number to which it corresponds. This will provide you with a set of 100 flash cards. Next, shuffle these cards thoroughly and go through the deck looking at each number. Try to remember which peg word goes with each number. Use the digit-consonant mnemonic to help you remember. The link mnemonic will also help. If you can't remember the peg word for 58, you may be able to remember the peg word for 57, and this will provide a cue for 58. Don't worry about how long it takes to remember. If you are sure that you cannot remember the word, then look at the peg word on the other side of the card. As you go through the cards, sort them into two groups; one for the cards you answered correctly and one for the cards you answered incorrectly. When you are finished with the deck of 100 cards, shuffle the smaller set of cards on which you made errors and sort these into correct and incorrect. Continue doing this until no cards are left in the incorrect pile. Now take all 100 cards, shuffle them, and go through the whole process again. When you know all 100 peg words, you should be able to give the peg word for any number within a couple of seconds. Review the list periodically so that the peg words will always be ready for use.

Exercise 5.6. If you think that you know the 100 peg words pretty well, memorize the following list of 100 items by associating each word in the list to the peg word that corresponds to its number. Take note of each composite containing the images of the two words for detail, color, and interaction. Go through the list twice before you try to recall the words just to make sure that you have a clear, interactive image for each peg word-item pair. A number of words on this list will be words that you may also use as peg words. For example, the first word on the list is *bell* which is my 95th peg word. When I get to the 95th peg word will I get the image for *tie/bell* or will I get the image for *bell/tractor,* or both? As was discussed in Chapter 3, there are two ways around this problem. First, whenever you recognize a list word as a peg word, use an image for the list word different from the image you usually use for the peg word. I always use the image of a church bell for *bell,* so for the list word *bell,* I can use the image of a doorbell. Later, if my image contains a church bell I will know that in that image *bell* is the peg word. A second way to keep peg words and list words distinct is to mentally paint a large X on the image that represents the list word. So if I have only one image for the word *bell,* then in the image for *tie/bell* the bell will have a large X painted on it. In the image for *bell/tractor,* the bell will be my usual image for the peg word *bell.*

1.	bell	11.	squirrel	21.	elephant	31.	bread
2.	anchor	12.	bee	22.	olive	32.	whale
3.	rail	13.	pimple	23.	truck	33.	knight
4.	bird	14.	skull	24.	church	34.	button
5.	moose	15.	napkin	25.	photograph	35.	grasshopper
6.	leaf	16.	tent	26.	head	36.	clown
7.	jelly	17.	palace	27.	cup	37.	girdle
8.	trombone	18.	cat	28.	horn	38.	nickel
9.	gate	19.	gun	29.	brick	39.	rat
10.	pail	20.	horse	30.	snake	40.	casket

41.	lion	56.	earthworm	71.	camel	86.	submarine
42.	violin	57.	spike	72.	glasses	87.	jockey
43.	screwdriver	58.	pearl	73.	kitten	88.	knob
44.	priest	59.	purse	74.	emerald	89.	mirror
45.	tweezer	60.	queen	75.	minnow	90.	feet
46.	jar	61.	jewel	76.	nun	91.	coal
47.	slipper	62.	propeller	77.	racket	92.	pigeon
48.	moon	63.	carpet	78.	cigarette	93.	skate
49.	typewriter	64.	medal	79.	dancer	94.	piano
50.	turtle	65.	nightgown	80.	butterfly	95.	pillow
51.	basket	66.	toaster	81.	missle	96.	tractor
52.	nurse	67.	envelope	82.	honey	97.	spoon
53.	cow	68.	bomb	83.	gorilla	98.	boot
54.	ham	69.	coat	84.	mattress	99.	pie
55.	saxophone	70.	steeple	85.	king	100.	pencil

Now write down the numbers 1 to 100 on a sheet of paper. Next to each number write down the corresponding word from the list.

Prices and model numbers

In business it is often convenient to memorize the prices or model numbers of various articles, especially when it becomes annoying to have to look up information repeatedly. Also, prices and model numbers provide us with a convenient way of practicing the digit-consonant mnemonic. Here are some examples using the digit-consonant mnemonic in conjunction with the link mnemonic to associate the price of an article with the article itself.

brush/$1.95

The digit 1 can be coded as *tie* and the number 95 as *bell* using the digit-consonant mnemonic. Use the link mnemonic to form a visual image of a brush painting a tie. Next, form a visual image of a bell hanging from the bottom of the tie and ringing. Later, if someone asks you the price of a brush, you can form the image of the tie and the bell and you will be able to decode the two numbers as 1 and 95.

You don't always have to use the 100 peg words. You can make up new words for the occasion. For example, 195 can be coded as *table,* and you could form the visual image of a brush painting a table. However, until you become experienced it may be easier to use the 100 peg words that you have available in memory. Another example is:

hunting bow/$54.85

Fifty-four can be coded as *lure* and 85 as *file.* I formed the mental image of a hunting bow shooting a fishing lure instead of an arrow, and the lure striking a file used to file wood or metal. For the item:

microscope/$349.99

the coding of 3, 49, and 99 are *Ma, rope,* and *pipe* respectively. The linking images could be: the microscope fell on Ma; Ma cut a piece of rope; and one end of the rope was tied to a pipe.

Exercise 5.7. Sometimes the sequence of digits 01, 02, etc. will appear in prices. So at this time go to the Appendix and choose a peg word for the digits 0, 00, 01, 02, 03, 04, 05, 06, 07, 08, and 09. Try to memorize these additional peg words right now. Make up a flashcard for each of these additional 11 numbers and add them to your deck of numbers and peg words.

*Exercise 5.8. The following list consists of ten articles and their prices. Memorize the price of each item by using first the digit-consonant mnemonic and then the link mnemonic on each item. Test yourself by writing down the list of articles in a random order and then writing the price next to each one.

1. shirt/$11.19
2. paint/$7.45
3. sofa/$575.00
4. skillet/$6.31
5. cannon/$1549.79
6. crown/$8750.90
7. bouquet/$4.96
8. hatchet/$6.29
9. spear/$21.10
10. globe/$25.65

A procedure similar to the one used for remembering the prices of goods can be used to remember model numbers. Let's say you had to remember the model number of the following piece of equipment:

Eastern Electronics stereo (small)/173-45A

The model number could be broken up into 1, 73, 45, and A. Here, using *both* the 100 peg word mnemonic and the alphabetic mnemonic, you get the sequence: *tie, comb, rail,* and *ape.* Then, using the link mnemonic, something like the following sequence of images might result: the small stereo has a red bow tie wrapped around it; a comb is being used to cut the bow tie; the comb is dropped and breaks on a railroad rail; a large ape is bending the rail.

Exercise 5.9. Use the digit-consonant mnemonic, the alphabet mnemonic and the link mnemonic to memorize the model numbers given for the following listed articles. Note each individual image for detail, color, and interaction. Test yourself by listing the articles in an order different from the way they are listed and writing the model number next to each.

1. garden shovel/39
2. metal barrel/75
3. steel chain/Z11
4. electric drill/12M
5. window fan/X64S
6. small rowboat/AK113
7. fishhooks/4157B
8. pencil sharpener/P80

chapter six

The keyword mnemonic

The technique to be discussed in this chapter, the keyword mnemonic, is a technique that is useful in a wide variety of situations. The essential characteristic of a keyword mnemonic is that it changes a meaningless signal or cue for remembering into a word that is meaningful. It is then easier to remember the relevant information related to the signal or cue. In the keyword mnemonic pegs and loci are not needed. We assume the cue for the information that you should remember is going to be presented to you. However, the big problem is that the cue is often not very meaningful. As an example of what this means, let's look at an early use of the keyword procedure: the memorization of the English equivalents of foreign-language vocabulary words. If you want to remember that the English meaning for the Spanish word *perro* (pronounced something like PEAR-oh) is *dog,* what would you do? In the keyword technique you would first try to think of an English word that sounds like *perro,* perhaps the word *pear.* Going from the meaningless word *perro* to an English word that sounds like it is called the *phonetic* link. Not only should this keyword sound like *perro,* but it should also be an English word that represents a concrete object and can be easily imaged. The reason for this is that in the next step, the *imagery* link, a visual image is formed containing a pear and a dog. For example a mental image may be formed of a big pear being eaten by a dog. Now, the next time the word *perro* is seen or heard, it should remind you of the keyword *pear* through the phonetic link. Forming a visual image of a pear will then give you the word *dog* through the imagery link.

Exercise 6.1.   The following list consists of Spanish nouns with their English equivalents. The words in parentheses will give you some idea of how these words are pronounced. Make up a keyword that sounds like the Spanish word (the phonetic link) and then make up a visual image using your keyword and the English equivalent of the Spanish word (the imagery link). Make sure you note each image for detail, color, and interaction.

> ropa (ROPE a)—clothes
> carta (CART a)—letter
> cabra (COB ra)—goat
> sopa (SOAP a)—soup
> zorro (ZOAR oh)—fox

The keyword mnemonic has been useful in helping people learn foreign language vocabulary. But it has many other uses. A few of these will now be discussed.

Historic dates

Let's say that you wanted to remember the following historic date:

Cortez conquered the Aztecs in 1519.

What is desired here is a way of remembering the date 1519 when the question is asked, "When did Cortez conquer the Aztecs?" You might even ask yourself this question if you are a student and are writing an answer on a history exam.

First, what should be the keyword? It certainly should be based on an important word in the historic date, but should it be based on the word *Cortez* in the statement or on the word *Aztec?* The answer to this question depends on a number of factors such as which word is more likely to be in the question if both are not. Another consideration is which word results in the best keyword. The importance of finding a keyword that will be remembered cannot be overemphasized. The important word in the statement of the historic fact from which the keyword is derived is known as the "cue word." Since the keyword is recalled from its "cue word" by the way the cue word sounds, choose a keyword that you know you will be reminded of when you later see or hear the cue word. There is no visual imagery to help you with this step. It is based primarily on phonetic association. For the cue word *Cortez* the words *court, cord,* or *quart* may be used as keywords. For the cue word *Aztec* the words *ax, ax* tag, or *ash tic* could be used. Let's use *court* as in *tennis court.* The word *court* may be a very logical choice as a keyword derived from *Cortez.* However, if you believe that it is a word that you will not remember when you hear the word *Cortez* then don't use it. If the first word you think of when you think of *Cortez* is *corpse,* then use that word as a keyword. The keyword must come automatically to you later on. Often the best keyword is the first word you think of. However, as was mentioned before, the keyword should represent a concrete object so that it can be easily imaged. Experience using these techniques greatly improves your skill with them. Keep working at it.

Now the date 1519 is easy. It can be encoded as *towel* (15) and *tub* (19) from the peg words that I chose in Chapter 5. *Cortez* becomes *court* through the phonetic link. The imagery link will actually consist of two linking visual images. The first links the image of a tennis court to the image of a towel. Perhaps you can form the image of a tennis court being wiped off with a towel. The second links a towel to a tub. Think of a towel being thrown into a tub.

Another example is:

Jamestown, Virginia was founded in 1607.

Here the keyword could be James with 1607 encoded as *dish* and sock. The two linking visual images could be: (1) a person you know named James holding a dish, (2) in the dish is a sock.

*Exercise 6.2.   For the following historic events and their years of occurrence, (1) Choose an important word describing the event, the cue word. (2) Create a keyword from the cue word. Make sure that the keyword is phonetically similar to the cue word and is easily imaged. (3) Encode the date using either the peg words from the 100 peg-word mnemonic or use words you make up. If you already know the century, encode only the last two digits, such as 33 for 1933. (4) Use the link mnemonic to connect the keywords and the words generated from the dates. (5) Note each image for detail, color, and interaction.

1. Spanish Armada defeated by the English—1588
2. Printing of the King James Bible—1611
3. Great Plague of London—1665
4. Philadelphia founded—1682
5. The Boston Massacre—1770

6. Battle of the Alamo—1836
7. Lincoln's Gettysburg Address—1863
8. Suez Canal opens—1869
9. Start of Prohibition in America—1917
10. Hitler becomes Chancellor of Germany—1933

Names and telephone numbers

The technique for associating a person's telephone number to his or her name is very much the same as memorizing historic dates, prices, or model numbers. For example, let's try to memorize the telephone number of Wilma Tuttle, which is 533-7012. Here are the four steps in the process:

1. Create a keyword or a key phrase from the person's name. It should be phonetically similar to the name and be easily imageable. In this example *Tuttle* might be changed to *turtle*.
2. Encode the telephone number using the peg words from the 100 peg word mnemonic. 53-3-70-12 could be transformed into *loom, Ma, case,* and *tin.*
3. Use the link mnemonic to chain together the keyword with the sequence of peg words. For example, the *turtle* was working at a *loom*. Sitting on the *loom* was *Ma. Ma* was holding a heavy *case*. In the heavy *case* were some *tin* cans.
4. Note each image for detail, color, and interaction.

Sometimes you may also wish to remember a person's last name as well as telephone number after becoming familiar with his or her first name. You might get to know Wilma, but have trouble remembering her last name Tuttle. In this situation you can form a separate keyword for the first and last name. Wilma could be coded as *willow*. Then the sequence of words in the link mnemonic would be *willow, turtle, loom, Ma, case,* and *tin.*

*Exercise 6.3. Create a mnemonic for each of the names and telephone numbers given below. Follow the preceding four-step process. Test yourself by writing down the names in a random order and then writing down the telephone numbers next to each one. Make up a separate keyword for the first and last name if you wish to. Otherwise create a keyword for only the last name.

1.	Oscar Knapp	655-3771
2.	Conrad Levinson	073-5180
3.	Calvin Collier	180-5707
4.	Beatrice Flanagan	604-9088
5.	Monica Friedlander	254-3951
6.	Ethel Applebaum	310-4838
7.	Sydney Bradley	007-4291
8.	Deborah Jasper	300-1275
9.	Ashley Saccoccia	336-5248
10.	Flora Reynolds	793-7562

Building your English vocabulary

How many times have you had the experience of reading a book or an article and coming across the same unfamiliar word time and time again? If you were feeling ambitious, you may have looked up the meaning of the word. So then what happened? You later came across the word again and couldn't remember its meaning. It's a frustrating experience, and many people just don't bother looking up words that they do not know. I think that we would all agree that some procedure is needed to help us remember the meanings of unfamiliar words after we look them up in the dictionary. Fortunately, the keyword method is an effective way for doing this, and it operates the same way as memorizing foreign language vocabulary discussed earlier in the chapter. The procedure, however, does require some effort on your part. Also, you have to have a dictionary.

Let's say that the word *ameliorate* is one that you come across in your reading, and it is a word whose meaning you would like to remember. Here are the steps needed in using the keyword mnemonic for building your English vocabulary:

1. Look up the word in a dictionary and find out how it is pronounced. *Ameliorate* is pronounced something like a-MEAL-yo-rate—the second syllable is accented.

2. Now look at the meanings of the word listed in the dictionary and choose the one that you want to remember. Often the last meaning listed is the most modern one. *Ameliorate* is a verb meaning *to make better; to improve.*

3. Use the pronunciation of *ameliorate* to create a keyword that is imageable and sounds like some part of *ameliorate*. The sounds used should come from the beginning of the word. For example, the keyword could be *meal.* For those of you with some foreign language training, a foreign word can be used as a keyword. For example, *ameliorate* is related to the Latin word *melior* meaning *better.* This is a good choice for the keyword if you know some Latin.

4. Create a sentence using the keyword and a set of words that defines, contains, or implies the meaning of the word that you are learning. For example, use the sentence, "The meal he ate made the starving man feel better." Try to make the words in the sentence represent concrete objects.

5. Form as vivid a visual image as you can of the sentence, concentrating on the keyword and a word in the sentence that defines, contains, or implies the meaning of the original word. If you have an image, take note of its detail, color, and interaction. Forming an image may not always be easy, because an abstract word such as *better* is not easily imaged.

Now, when you later come across the word *ameliorate,* the following events should take place: You should pronounce the word correctly to yourself. Next, you should think of the keyword *meal* from the pronunciation. Then you should be able to form a visual image of the meal, the starving man, and the meal making him feel better. You should then remember that the word *ameliorate* means *to make better; to improve.*

Let's try another example; the word *equivocate.*

1. Its pronunciation is ee-KWIV-oh-kate.
2. One of its primary meanings is *to lie*, or *to not tell the truth.*
3. In this example two keywords will be used, *quiver:Kate,* each of which is phonetically similar to a syllable in the word *equivocate.* Having two keywords may be helpful to you if you are learning a large number of words at any one time and are having trouble remembering which keyword goes with each new word.
4. The mnemonic could be the sentence, "The man with the quiver of arrows is lying to Kate."
5. Form a visual image of the quiver of arrows, Kate, and the man lying to Kate. Note the image for detail, color, and interaction.

If you are interested in improving your English vocabulary in a systematic way, you might start a notebook listing your newly acquired words alphabetically along with their keywords and mnemonic sentences. You could then occasionally review these newly learned words and their associated keywords, mnemonics, and meanings. When you think you know a word well enough, remove it from your list. You should no longer need the mnemonic to remember its meaning. A way of organizing the parts of the mnemonic is given in the next exercise.

*Exercise 6.4.   Create keyword mnemonics for the following twelve words even if you already know the meanings of some of them. Make five columns on a sheet of paper. Label these columns (1) *word,* (2) *pronunciation,* (3) *meaning,* (4) *keyword,* and (5) *mnemonic sentence.* Fill in each of the columns after you look up the pronunciation and meaning of each word.

1. implacable	7. tacit
2. fetish	8. adipose
3. gullible	9. extirpate
4. rancor	10. ignominy
5. hegemony	11. harbinger
6. magnate	12. jejune

Spelling mnemonics

Almost all of us have trouble spelling certain words. Often these words are fairly simple, frequently occurring words, but for one reason or another they are often misspelled. For me two such words are *across* and *resistance.* I have a strong inclination to spell *across* with two Cs and to spell *resistance* with *ence.* Everybody has their own spelling demons, but not surprisingly the same words often cause trouble for many people. Unless a conscious effort is made to correct the way we have these problem words stored in our memory, we will continue to make the same spelling errors over and over again. One way to break these bad habits is to form a spelling mnemonic for each of the words that we are misspelling.

The keyword mnemonic can also be used to help you remember the correct spelling of those words that you find difficult to spell. For example, let's say that I want to remember how to spell *across* with one C rather than two. Using the keyword mnemonic, follow these steps:

1. Create a keyword or key phrase that is phonetically similar to the word to be spelled. Try to make the keyword or key phrase represent concrete objects that can be mentally pictured. For *across,* I may form the keyword *cross.*
2. Form a sentence using the keyword and other words. These other words should contain the same letter sequences as those found in the word that you are trying to spell. Concentrate on finding words that contain the same letter sequences that make the word difficult for you to spell. Try to make as many of these words as possible represent concrete objects. For example, for the word *across* I use the sentence "I see *a cross.*" Sometimes, adding the word to be spelled to the sentence is possible and may help you remember the sentence, such as, "I see *a cross across* the street."
3. Form as good an image as possible from the mnemonic sentence so that you will think of the image when you hear the keyword.
4. Note your image for detail, color, and interaction.

What about the word *resistance?* My keyword for *resistance* is *tan,* and my mnemonic sentence is, "The resis*tan*ce soldiers wore *tan* uniforms." My keyword for *misspell* is *Miss Pell.* The sentence that I use is, *"Miss Pell,* a bright person like you shouldn't *misspell* words."

Sometimes spelling mnemonics are very difficult to create. You may be better off simply trying to remember the spelling of the word by memorizing the letters directly. This is the best example that I could come up with for the word *auxiliary* which I tend to spell in many different ways.

> auxiliary:auto—the *au*to was *X*-rayed; *I* am a *liar.*

Here is a more successful example that keeps me from adding an *e* to *gu* for *argument.*

> argument:gum—Stop this ar*gum*ent about *gum.*

Note that in this example the keyword *gum* really doesn't sound like any part of the word *argument,* so it may be harder to remember the keyword *gum* than a keyword more phonetically similar to *argument.* But *gum* was the best that I could do.

Here are four more examples to give you a better idea of how spelling mnemonics work. The italicized letters in the word are the letters difficult to remember.

> villain:villa—The vill*ai*n was *in* the vill*a.*
> business:sin—Bu*sin*ess is no *sin.*
> piece:pie—I want a *pie*ce of *pie.*
> annual:Ann—*Ann,* yo*u,* and *Al* are invited to the *annual* picnic.

*Exercise 6.5. You may or may not know how to spell the words in the next list. But as an exercise do the following: (1) choose a keyword or key phrase phonetically similar to the word to be spelled. Try to choose a word for which a visual image can be formed. (2) Create a sentence using the keyword and other words that contain the sequence of letters used in the correct spelling of the word. The letter sequences that are italicized indicate where most spelling errors occur. Concentrate on finding words that include these difficult letter sequences. Try to choose high-imagery words. As in the preceding examples, form the following columns on a sheet of paper: the word to be spelled, the keyword, and the mnemonic sentence. (3) Try to create a visual image from the sentence that will be cued by the keyword. (4) Note your image for detail, color, and interaction, although the sentences used as spelling mnemonics often may not contain a large amount of visual imagery.

1. marri*a*ge
2. am*o*ng
3. w*ei*rd
4. tra*g*edy
5. d*e*sp*air*
6. shep*h*erd
7. par*all*el
8. d*ea*lt
9. nick*el*
10. s*ei*ze

When you write and use a word whose spelling you are unsure of, look it up in the dictionary and immediately try to create a spelling mnemonic for it. What letters were you uncertain of? Concentrate on finding words containing those letters. If you are an especially poor speller, it might be worthwhile to start a spelling notebook in which you can write your mnemonics so that you can periodically review them.

Using the story mnemonic in spelling

For some groups of words it may not be a good idea to form a separate spelling mnemonic for each word using the keyword procedure. For example, some words end in *ence* and some words end in *ance*. Two similar suffixes also occur as *ent* and *ant*. No other part of the word may cause spelling difficulty except the ending. Rather than trying to deal with each word separately, it may be easier to organize these words into sets and connect the words with the same suffixes using the story mnemonic. Then, if you are unsure whether a word ends in *ance* or *ence,* run through your *ant* story. If the word or some variation of it occurs in the *ant* story, then it ends in either *ance* or *ant*. Otherwise it ends in *ence* or *ent*. Of course, the hundreds of words ending in *ant* cannot be placed in a story, so for this example I have chosen the words that are most commonly misspelled. When you make up a story, you would include only those words that *you* have trouble spelling. Many of the following words might be replaced with others, and a different story made up.

THE ANTICS OF AN ANT

The *pleasant* ant put on a *brilliant performance.* The *attendance* at his *appearance* was *predominantly* people of *importance.* Many old *acquaintances* who sought *admittance* at the *entrance* were turned away. The ant's ego soon became a *hindrance,* and his *acceptance* of *guidance* was impossible. He now acted *ignorant* and *dominant.* It is *significant* that there soon was a *warrant* for his arrest.

Exercise 6.6. Make up stories for the following sets of words. First go through each list and cross out the words you are sure that you already know how to spell and do not include these in your story. You can include the words in your story in any order that you want.

Set 1: altar, angular, beggar, burglar, calendar, caterpillar, cedar, cellar, circular, collar, curricular, dollar, familiar, grammar, hangar, insular, jugular, liar, lunar, molar, muscular, nectar, particular, peculiar, pillar, polar, popular, regular, scholar, similar, singular, spectacular, sugar, vehicular, vinegar, vulgar.

Set 2: accelerator, actor, administrator, aggressor, anchor, auditor, author, aviator, bachelor, behavior, benefactor, cantor, collector, commentator, competitor, conqueror, contributor, councilor, counselor, creditor, debtor, dictator, director, distributor, doctor, editor, educator, elevator, emperor, escalator, executor, factor, governor, harbor, humor, inferior, inventor, investigator, janitor, legislator, manor, minor, mortgagor, motor, neighbor, odor, pastor, prior, professor, protector, radiator, sailor, sculptor, senator, suitor, supervisor, tenor, traitor, ventilator, visitor.

chapter seven

The first-letter mnemonic

In previous chapters a number of lists of peg-words were presented so that a large number of high-imagery structures would be available in memory for the storage of new information. These systems included the rhyming peg words, the alphabet peg words, the 100 loci, and the 100 peg words derived from the numbers 1 to 100. These pegs *on the walls of your memory closet* are to be used over and over again, with the older information stored on the pegs replaced by the more recently learned information. However, what if there is some information that you wish to remember permanently? Should you use some of your available pegs or loci to store this information? Based on the small amount of research evidence available, this is a difficult question to answer. Some experts on mnemonics believe that you can use the same set of peg words to remember a variety of word lists simultaneously and recall any particular list you want. Recall is successful because the different lists are learned in different contexts and therefore don't interfere with each other. However, we shall play it safe and assume that a newly learned set of words interferes with the recall of the older sets of words learned with the same pegs.

In this chapter we discuss a technique by which information can be stored permanently in memory and not be wiped out by newer information. The system is quite simple. You simply create a special set of peg words that you will use only for the information you wish to remember permanently. Since you will be creating peg words that will be used only for one set of information, no later information will interfere with what you have already stored. Perhaps your first reaction is to think that this system is a bit crazy. Why create and memorize a new set of peg words to which the important information can be attached? Wouldn't it always be easier to simply memorize the information you think is important and not fool with additional peg-word systems? The answer is no! Sometimes it is easier to create special sets of peg words. The reasons for this will become more apparent as we proceed.

Sometimes information can be directly remembered by casting it into the form of a rhyme. In this system there are no peg words, because the words of the rhyme themselves represent what you want to remember. By using a rhyme you are increasing the association among the words and ensuring that you will be able to remember them. One example of this is the rhyme for remembering the number of days in each month of the year that many of us learned in grade school:

> *Thirty days has September,*
> *April, June, and November.*
> *All the rest have thirty-one*
> *Except February.*

It alone has twenty-eight
And one day more one year in four.

Another rhyme mnemonic aids us in spelling.

I *before* E *except after* C
Or when sounded like A
As in "reindeer" or "sleigh"
Or when sounded like I
As in "heigh-ho" or "stein."

However, information that we would like to remember cannot always be cast into the form of a rhyme. It is sometimes easier to remember information permanently by creating a special peg-word system for it. The following procedures can be used to make the peg words and the information attached to them easier to remember. First, choose peg words that are already related to one another and thus easier to remember. Second, choose peg words that are related to the information you wish to remember. A common way of doing this is to choose a sequence of peg words that have the same first letters as the corresponding words in the list that you wish to remember. If remembering the special peg words and their relation to the material is easier than remembering the material in its original form, then this mnemonic will save time in learning and result in more accurate recall.

Using first letters as cues

The memory technique that is of primary interest in this chapter is the first-letter mnemonic. Researchers have found that the first-letter mnemonic is the most popular mnemonic used spontaneously by college students. There are two steps in using the first-letter mnemonic. First, to memorize a list of words write down the first letter of each word after arranging the words in the order that you want to remember them. Sometimes the first letters themselves can be formed into a meaningful word. The word *HOMES* gives the first letters of the names of the Great Lakes: Huron, Ontario, Michigan, Erie, and Superior. The states that border the Great Lakes are New York, Pennsylvania, Ohio, Indiana, Michigan, Illinois, Wisconsin, and Minnesota. Rearranging the first letters of these states gives you a mnemonic such as *I'M NO WIMP.*

Most often the first letters cannot be formed into a word or sentence. This is especially true if the words are in a particular order and cannot be moved around. So the second step is to choose words that start with the same letters and also seem to go together to form a memorable sentence or phrase. Here is an example:

Men Very Easily Make Jugs Serve Useful Nocturnal Purposes.

The first letter in each word of the sentence represents the first letters of the names of the planets in their order from the sun: Mercury, Venus, Earth, Mars, Jupiter, Saturn, Uranus, Neptune, and Pluto. As you might expect, it helps to use words that are easily imageable so that you can remember an image as well as a sentence. Another choice for remembering the planets is the sentence:

My Very Excellent Mom Just Served Us Nice Pickles.

The following example consists of a list of the original thirteen American colonies in the order that they voted to ratify the Constitution. Because three of the states start with the word *New* (New Jersey, New Hampshire, and New York), we will take the first letter for these states from the words Jersey, Hampshire, and York and use the first-letter mnemonic to memorize this list.

1. Delaware
2. Pennsylvania
3. New Jersey
4. Georgia

5. Connecticut
6. Massachusetts
7. Maryland
8. South Carolina
9. New Hampshire

10. Virginia
11. New York
12. North Carolina
13. Rhode Island

You may notice that in this list two names of states start with the letter M even after the word *new* was eliminated. This is not an uncommon occurrence in any list of thirteen words, and it points to one of the limitations of the first-letter mnemonic. Massachusetts comes before Maryland. You simply have to remember this. Note that they are *not* in alphabetical order. Maybe this fact will help you remember their correct order. Now let's try to make up a sentence containing words that have the same first letters as the states and occur in the same order. How about the following:

Delaware Patriots Joyfully Give Consent Making More State Houses Vote "Yes," Nourishing Ratification.

This sentence means something to me, but it may not be very meaningful to you, so try to make up your own. In making up this sentence I used the first letter from the name of each state to create a corresponding peg word in the sentence that started with the same letter. However, I also tried to make the meaning of the sentence related in some way to the meaning of the list. The list represents the order in which the thirteen American colonies ratified the United States Constitution. The first state in the list is also part of the mnemonic sentence. Using a word from the list in the sentence may also help you to remember the mnemonic sentence.

Now let's try to recall the states from the mnemonic. The first word is *Delaware* and stands for Delaware. The second word is *Patriots* and stands for Pennsylvania. The third word is *Joyfully* and stands for New Jersey. You may have noticed something unusual in this procedure. What has happened to association using visual imagery? We may try to utilize visual imagery to remember the sentence, but we don't use it to recall the states once we have remembered the words in the mnemonic sentence. What is relied upon primarily is our familiarity with the names of the eastern American States. We know these names well enough so that the first letter of each name is an effective cue for the name of the corresponding state. First letters would not be effective cues using visual imagery unless the letters were encoded using the alphabet peg words (Chapter 3), and this was not done. So the first-letter mnemonic, as it is being used here, has another limitation: the words being recalled should be already familiar as a group, whether the group be planets or American States. There are some ways to get around these limitations, and these will be discussed later in the chapter.

In summary the first-letter mnemonic is easy to use, and it is frequently used. But it has some limitations. They are: (1) The list cannot be too long. If it is, then you may have trouble making up a long meaningful sentence. (2) Most of the time more than one word will start with the same letter. If you are trying to remember words in their correct order, you will simply have to remember which of the items in the list with the same first letter appears first. (3) Visual imagery is not used for forming associations between the letters and the words because the words that should be remembered are already familiar as a group.

*Exercise 7.1. This exercise consists of a list of the first nine presidents of the United States. Create a first-letter mnemonic to remember their names in the correct order. Use as many concrete words as possible so that the sentence can be more easily recalled. Also, use words that are related to the topic of "Early Presidents" so that you can associate the mnemonic sentence with the topic. Make up a sentence that is meaningful and memorable to *you.*

1. Washington
2. Adams (John)
3. Jefferson
4. Madison
5. Monroe
6. Adams (John Quincy)
7. Jackson
8. Van Buren
9. Harrison

Exercise 7.2.   Following is a list of the eleven Confederate States in the order that they seceded from the Union at the start of the American Civil War. Use the first-letter mnemonic to memorize the names of these states in order. Note that two of the states have names that start with the letter A and two have names that start with the letter T.

1. South Carolina
2. Mississippi
3. Florida
4. Alabama
5. Georgia
6. Louisiana
7. Texas
8. Virginia
9. Arkansas
10. North Carolina
11. Tennessee

*Exercise 7.3.   Unless you are a lover of poetry, the names listed below of well-known English Romantic poets are probably not very familiar to you. The poets are listed in approximately the same chronological order in which they lived. Try to memorize the last names on this list in one of two ways. If you are familiar with these names, then memorize the list using the first-letter mnemonic. If you are not familiar with these names, then use the word substitution technique discussed in Chapter 4 in conjunction with one of the peg-word systems to memorize the list.

1. Robert Burns
2. William Blake
3. William Wordsworth
4. Samuel Taylor Coleridge
5. Sir Walter Scott
6. Lord Byron
7. Percy Bysshe Shelley
8. John Keats

*Exercise 7.4.   In this exercise I hope that I will be able to show you that the first-letter mnemonic doesn't work with unfamiliar words. But maybe it will work for you anyway, and you'll confound me. The following list consists of the names of eight of the most famous painters of the High Renaissance in the sixteenth century. They are listed in approximately the same chronological order in which they lived and influenced one another. Nearly everybody has heard of Leonardo da Vinci, but some of the other names are less familiar. Use the first-letter mnemonic if you think you can, otherwise make up substitute words for these unfamiliar names and use one of the peg-word systems or perhaps the link mnemonic to memorize the list. I have placed some approximate pronunications in parentheses next to each name to help you if you are making up substitute words.

1. Leonardo da Vinci—(Leon-ARE-doe da VIN-chee)
2. Michelangelo—(Michael-AN-jello)
3. Raphael—(Raff-ee-el)
4. Giorgione—(Jor-JOAN-knee)
5. Titian—(TISH-en)
6. Correggio—(Core-REJ-oh)
7. Durer—(DYOUR-er)
8. Holbein—(HOLE-bine)

The first-letter mnemonic is used to memorize information that will be retained permanently, or at least for a long period of time. You may have to review the mnemonic occasionally to make sure that you don't forget it. However, the fact that you may not easily forget a mnemonic can also be a cause for concern. What if you continue to deal with this information frequently or are exposed to it regularly? Will the mnemonic continue to clutter up your mind and not go away? Fortunately, this is not the case. As you become more familiar with material you first learned mnemonically, the mnemonic will gradually fade away unless you make it a point to review it. If you use this information in a meaningful way and learn more about how it relates to other information, then more direct associations will be created between the items to be remembered, and a more natural organization of the information will develop in memory.

chapter eight

Remembering names and faces

It may be because of their line of work, or it may simply be because of their interest in other people, whatever the reason there are many individuals who are very interested in being able to remember the name that goes with a familiar face. This interest is understandable. The professional success of many men and women depends partly on being able to remember names and other information about people after meeting them only once. Even if your work doesn't depend on this skill, it often helps to be able to call people you have recently met by their first names. It can be embarrassing to try to talk to someone about whom you remember absolutely nothing, yet whose face is very familiar.

There are three basic problems that have to be dealt with

by any face-name mnemonic: (1) *Lack of time*. Often, such as in a social gathering, a dozen or more people may be introduced to you in the course of a few minutes. You may try to slow the pace of new introductions, but often you are forced to associate faces and names as best you can. (2) *Encoding of names*. Some last names such as Hill, Archer, King, and Post represent concrete objects that can be visualized and remembered. But many last names such as Conners, Pauling, or Warner, are abstract words to most people and do not represent anything that can be visualized. Some last names such as Bain, Gato, Bruno, or Vetter represent meaningful words in other languages, but this is of little help unless you happen to know what the meanings of those words are. Being able to form visual images of objects associated with names is as important in the face-name mnemonic as it is in other mnemonics. (3) *Encoding of faces*. The face of any person is distinct and meaningful. Often we can recognize a person as somebody we have seen before, even if that meeting was brief and happened a long time ago. The main problem is that a face is a meaningful visual pattern but not a meaningful verbal pattern. Until we do something to transform or encode a person's face, we won't be able to associate a person's name to his or her face. Of course, the association of names and faces does occur naturally. We probably can give the names to pictures of faces of hundreds of our friends, relatives, and public and historical figures. However, if we are to remember a fairly large number of new names and faces in a relatively short period of time, then a mnemonic procedure is helpful. The two procedures to be described here for associating names to faces both use some *distinctive feature* of a person's face to help recall his or her name.

Basic steps in associating faces and first names

The procedure for memorizing only a person's first name is the easier of the two procedures to be described, and it is one that many people naturally use when they try to memorize somebody's first name. The mnemonic is based on the idea that if you can associate the new person with someone you already know who has the same first name, then you will be more likely to remember the new person's first name. Let's use an example and go through the three basic steps.

1. You are introduced to a man named John Rafferty, and you want to remember his first name. Initially, you must make sure that you heard his name correctly. If you did not hear both his first and last name distinctly, then ask him or the person introducing you to say it again. This is usually not a problem because most people feel that you are sincerely interested in them if you attempt to get their name exactly right.

2. Many first names are very common, and the person you meet may have the same first name as somebody that you already know. For example, if you already know somebody named John Smith, then form a visual image of the face of John Smith and compare it to the face of the man you just met, John Rafferty.

3. Next, try to pick out some feature of John Rafferty's face that reminds you of your old friend John Smith. There is usually something about a new acquaintance's face that has some relation to any face that you are already familiar with. For example, your new friend John Rafferty may have an unusual nose just as does your old friend John Smith, even though their noses look very different from one another. Other characteristics about a person may remind you of your old friend with the same name. It could be the person's stature or mannerisms, or the way he or she talks. Remember that you can also associate first names with public or historical figures. If you meet somebody with the first name Abraham, think of Abraham Lincoln and how something about the person you just met reminds you of Abraham Lincoln.

Exercise 8.1. The following list consists of ten common first names for men and ten common first names for women. Try to form a visual image of the face and figure of an acquaintance, public figure, or historical personage with the same first name. If you can do this, then you probably will be able to visualize each of these people when meeting a new acquaintance with the same first name.

Men		*Women*	
1.	John	1.	Mary
2.	Bob	2.	Sue
3.	Bill	3.	Ann
4.	Jim	4.	Jane
5.	Tom	5.	Judy
6.	Joe	6.	Carol
7.	Dick	7.	Barb
8.	Mike	8.	Cathy
9.	George	9.	Linda
10.	Jack	10.	Joan

Exercise 8.2. The following exercise consists of photos of eight faces. By each photo is printed the person's first name. Using the first-name mnemonic, form a visual image of someone you know who has the same first name. Then find some feature of the face in the photo that is similar or related in some way to the face of the person you already know. Study each picture for at least fifteen seconds. After you do this for all eight photos, turn to page 92, which contains the photos but no names, look at each photo, and write down the person's first name.

Basic steps in associating faces and last names

Associating a person's face with his or her last name is usually more difficult than trying to learn only his or her first name. You'll see why this is true as we go through this next example.

Robin

John

Doris

Mark

Cathy

James

Linda

Paul

1. You have just met Mary Hamilton, and you would like to remember her last name, *Hamilton*. As in the procedure with first names, make sure that you hear both her first and last name correctly when you are introduced. The last name, *Hamilton*, does not represent any concrete object that can be visualized, so it will have to be encoded just as any abstract word is phonetically encoded (Chapter 4); that is, by substituting phonetically similar concrete nouns. Perhaps *Hamilton* can be encoded as *hammer:tin*.

2. The last name of the person should be encoded before studying the face. Otherwise, the name might be easily forgotten. The next step is to look carefully at the person's face or figure and try to find some distinctive feature to be used as a cue for his or her name. If possible, try to choose some permanent feature that will be recognizable the next time you meet that person rather than utilizing something that may change such as clothing or jewelry. Mary Hamilton may have eyebrows that are rather thick. If you decide to use this characteristic of her face, then make up a visual image of her eyebrows becoming even larger and thicker than they actually are, perhaps covering half of her face. This will help you recognize her eyebrows as the distinctive feature of her face the next time you meet her.

3. The final step is to try to associate the distinctive feature of Mary Hamilton's face with the encoding of her name. Try to form a visual image of her thick eyebrows as two hammer heads. Visualize these hammers as flattening a tin can that is resting between them on Mary Hamilton's nose. This may not be the particular image that you would form, but you would use whatever image comes to mind. Make sure you note your image for detail, color, and interaction, so that it becomes fixed in your mind.

4. An additional step may be possible, and you should include this additional step whenever you can. If you meet this person again at the same event or on that same day, then make sure you review the mnemonic for his or her name, even though

you had no trouble remembering the correct name at the time. This repetition will help you to retain the face-name association.

The next time you meet the Mary Hamilton of this example and look carefully at her face, you should instantly recognize her thick eyebrows as the distinctive feature that you used as a cue for her last name. Next, you should automatically remember the visual image of the hammers her eyebrows represent smashing a tin can. This *hammer:tin* combination should be an effective phonetic cue for the name *Hamilton*.

Will these bizarre images be forever engraved on your mind? If you get to know Mary Hamilton as a good friend, will you still be looking at her face years later and seeing hammers and tin cans? Don't worry, this shouldn't happen. These mnemonic images will eventually drop from memory when you get to know the person and a name will be learned.

*Exercise 8.3.   Use the phonetic encoding mnemonic to transform the following list of last names into nouns representing concrete objects.

1.	Webb	7.	Fraser
2.	Malone	8.	Collier
3.	Flanagan	9.	Gibson
4.	Pincelli	10.	Pinkham
5.	Riedel	11.	Sayre
6.	Tuttle	12.	Lawrence

You may have already asked yourself whether the two mnemonics that have been discussed can both be used at the same time. This is certainly possible, although it takes added time and effort on your part. If you have the time, try to use both the first-name and the last-name mnemonic. The same distinctive feature may be used for both mnemonics. Once you find a distinctive feature of your new acquaintance that reminds you of somebody with the same first name, use this same distinctive feature and associate it with some encoding of his or her last name. If it turns out that a person's first name is unfamiliar, then you will have to encode the first name in the same way as you encoded the last. For example, if you met a man with the name *Algernon Norris*, the whole name might be encoded as the word sequence, *ale, German, horse,* and images of this sequence would be associated to some distinctive feature of Mr. Norris' face using the link mnemonic (Chapter 2).

Remember that it often is not necessary to try to remember both names of a person. You might want to call people by their first names and not worry about what their last names are. Or, you might want to remember everybody as Mr., Mrs., or Ms. So-and-so. In these situations the use of a distinctive-feature mnemonic as a means of remembering face and name combinations is considerably easier. This is because only a first or last name, but not both, has to become associated with a face. In situations where you are pressed for time, you might want to concentrate on remembering first or last names, whichever is easier for each person you meet. If you later remember one name correctly, you may automatically remember the other. Also, when pressed for time, become an opportunist in choosing distinctive features. Use jewelry, clothing, glasses, anything that will help you remember a name over a period of an hour or two. Perhaps you will come across the person again a short time later, and in that case you may try to elaborate your mnemonic and incorporate into it a more permanent feature of the eyes, eyebrows, nose, ears, mouth, lips, teeth, chin, cheeks, forehead, skin, hairstyle, hands, hips, or bust: whatever is distinctive. Try not to use the same feature, such as a nose, for more than one or two people in a short period of time. In this way you can avoid confusing the names of people for whom you choose similar facial features.

*Exercise 8.4. The following exercise consists of photos of eight faces. Printed by each face is the name that goes with it. Using the distinctive-feature mnemonic, associate the last name with each face. The steps you should use are: (1) Pronounce and phonetically encode the name. (2) Find some distinctive feature to be used as a cue for the name. (3) Form a visual image of the distinctive facial feature and the transformed last name interacting. Note the images for detail, color, and interaction. Try to spend at least one minute coding and imaging each name and face. If you are feeling ambitious, you may try to memorize both the first and the last names at the same time. Now test yourself by writing down the complete names of each of the following pictured individuals.

The distinctive-feature mnemonic like all mnemonics becomes easier to use with practice. As you continue to use this mnemonic and look for distinctive features, use the phonetic substitution mnemonic for names, and use visual imagery for association, the entire process should become faster and more reliable. With experience you may notice that certain steps in the mnemonic don't seem to work well for you. If this occurs, make an effort to correct and improve the procedure you use. A common problem is to use substitute words in encoding the last name that are meaningful but not of high-imagery value. Later, these substitute words will be difficult to recall because they were not represented by visual images. If you become skilled at remembering people's first names, then make sure that you work next on remembering *both* first and last names. Your ultimate capabilities lie far beyond the level at which you start.

Debra Smelter

Mike Vest

Kathy Spangler

Keith Rothman

Gloria Philpot

Vernon Birteker

Brian Wolfe

Lotta Fischerstrom

chapter nine

Remembering prose material: the cue-word technique

The oldest known mnemonic technique, the method of loci, was used by orators in classical times not only to memorize lists of words but to memorize speeches as well. Even today students, teachers, clerics, and other professional men and women are interested not only in remembering lists of words and digits but in remembering the contents of a talk or speech that they have to present or the contents of a paper, article, or book chapter that they have read. If you are a college student, you may want to remember some set of information because you will later be tested on it. Or, for your own satisfaction you may want to review this information in your mind to try to better understand its implications and better integrate it with previous knowledge. We certainly want to comprehend the content of prose material, but sometimes it is also helpful to remember it in some detail. This task is often difficult, even when the material is well understood.

The method to be used here to increase retention of prose material is the *cue-word method*. The cue-word method is a method of outlining prose material in such a way that the outline is both effective for later recall and easy memorization. The steps in the cue-word method will be described first, and then we will go through an example. These are the steps you should go through in using the cue-word method.

1. Read through the material carefully. Make sure that you understand everything that you wish to remember. This first step is the most important step in the procedure. As you read the material, try to comprehend it. Form visual images to represent some of the information. By doing this you are actually memorizing parts of the passage. Remember that you will create problems for yourself when using the cue-word method if you try to memorize written material that you do not understand. If the material is difficult, you may have to read it more than once.

2. As you read the passage, write down possible cue words that can be used later to help you recall the passage. Cue words should be particularly important words from the text which you believe will help you remember other information that they are associated with. Cue words can be technical terms, names of concepts, people, places, and things; even numbers.

3. As you write down the cue words, draw a line whenever you start a new topic in the material. This provides you with a rough idea of the number of different subtopics in the passage.

4. When you are finished reading the material and have written down many possible cue words, go back through your list and decide how many cue words you would like to keep.

The number of cue words you keep depends on a number of factors. It depends most of all on how much of the material you wish to commit to memory. Make sure that you keep those cue words associated with the information you definitely want to remember and eliminate the others. Another factor that determines which cue words to keep and which to eliminate is how well you already know some of the information in the passage. If there is a paragraph, or even a page in a book, containing information that you already know fairly well, you may need only one cue word for it. Once the cue word gets you started, you will remember the associated information with no other prompting.

5. For each abstract cue word, use the phonetic substitution mnemonic to encode it into one or more concrete words. For each cue that is a number use the digit-consonant mnemonic to transform the number into a series of concrete words.

6. Use the link mnemonic, or one of the sets of pegs or loci, to memorize the cue words. Then, when you wish to reconstruct the material, recall your cue words and use them as prompters for the information in the passage that they are associated with.

7. If you have the time, wait a day or two and then review the mnemonic that was used to memorize the cue words. This will provide you with feedback indicating where possible forgetting may be occurring so that you can review the material and recreate your visual images. The review will also have the effect of further fixing the whole chain of images in your memory.

Using the cue-word mnemonic on short passages

As an example of the use of the cue-word technique, let's try to remember the following short passage which describes the bagpipe. This passage could be part of a longer text having to do with musical instruments.

THE BAGPIPE

The bagpipe is a very interesting musical instrument and is the national instrument of Scotland. It consists of a leather bag fitted with five wooden pipes. The player blows air into the bag through the blowpipe. Another pipe called the chanter has eight finger holes on which the melody is played. There are three drone pipes; each drone pipe plays a different fixed note. The player holds the bag under one arm and his arm pressure pushes the air through the four sounding pipes as he blows into the blowpipe. The bagpipe is used both as a solo instrument and in military bands. It is used in France, Ireland, India, and Spain as well as in Scotland. Even the ancient Romans used a form of bagpipe.

The information in this passage is probably unfamiliar to most people, but it is easily understood. Most people probably have to read it only once or twice in order to come up with a list of cue words. The list of cue words that I came up with are the following:

    Scotland
    five
    blowpipe
    chanter
    eight
    drone
    solo
    India
    Rome

The passage about the bagpipe was so short that I didn't draw any lines to group together cue words for different subtopics. Next, I wrote out the information from the passage that each cue word acted as a prompter for. This is the information that I associate with each cue word. Usually you wouldn't have to do this, but I want to give you an idea of how the cue words that I chose are working for me.

Scotland—the bagpipe is the national instrument of Scotland.

five—The bagpipe has five wooden pipes although it is made of leather.

blowpipe—The player blows into the bag through the blowpipe.

chanter—The chanter is the pipe that has holes in it and is fingered.

eight—The chanter has eight finger holes.

drone—The other three pipes are called drones and each drone plays a different note that never changes

solo—The bagpipe can be played as a solo instrument or as part of a military band.

India—The bagpipe is played in India, Ireland, France, and Spain as well as in Scotland.

Rome—A form of bagpipe was also known in ancient Rome.

Next, the cue words have to be transformed into words that can be linked together using visual imagery.

bagpipe—(name of topic)

Scotland—a Scot

five—owl (use the list of 100 peg words for digit-consonant encoding from Chapter 5)

blowpipe—bubble pipe

chanter—chanter (somebody who chants or sings)

eight—ivy (digit-consonant mnemonic, Chapter 5)

drone—drone (pilotless airplane)

solo (band)—a military band

India—Indian

Rome—image of the Colosseum

Now, the link mnemonic (Chapter 5) can be used to link together the images created from each cue word, where the cue words are chained together two at a time. Note for detail, color, and interaction.

bagpipe/Scot—Image a bagpipe being played by a Scot.

Scot/owl—Picture an owl sitting on the Scot's head.

owl/bubble pipe—Visualize the owl blowing bubbles out through a pipe.

bubble pipe/chanter—One bubble contains a chanter trying to sing.

chanter/ivy—The chanter is pulling off ivy growing on him.

ivy/drone—Visualize ivy growing over three drone airplanes.

drone/band—In each drone airplane there is a military band.

band/Indian—Each military band is made up of red Indian musicians.

Indian/Colosseum—The Indians are running around in the Colosseum.

Now, when you wish to recall the information about the bag-pipe in the correct order, simply go through the images of your link mnemonic and use the images to create the cue words. Each cue word should result in one or more sentences if you are writing or an idea that you can elaborate on if you are speaking. It should be noted that if you are to use the information organized by the cue-word mnemonic over and over, the material may take on a more natural structure of its own. This is true of any material that you study and work with over a period of time. But don't slight the cue-word technique. It is useful in helping you organize and remember material that you may want to use only once, and it acts as an aid to organize and remember material that in the long run you will come to know quite well.

*Exercise 9.1. After reading the following short passage about W. C. Fields, use the cue word technique to reconstruct from memory most of the information in the passage. Use steps one through seven listed at the beginning of this chapter to create your list of cue words.

W. C. FIELDS

W. C. Fields was one of the most popular comedians of his time and is still popular today. Many of his movies can be seen on television. Entertainers and impressionists still include his voice and speech patterns in their routines, and you sometimes hear his voice on television commercials. Fields was born in 1879 in Philadelphia as Claude William Dunkenfield and died in 1946. He started show business at an early age and first became a success as a juggler. Although he performed both on stage and on radio, he is best known as a film comedian. His best films include *You Can't Cheat an Honest Man* (1939), *My Little Chickadee* (1940), and *Never Give a Sucker an Even Break* (1941). Fields created a character that was unique in American film. He was cantankerous and witty. He exhibited a great deal of false courage, but feared and disliked dogs and even small children. The characters he played violated social mores in a rather deliberate manner at a time when few comic characters on the screen did so. He delighted in playing the role of a slightly drunken misfit.

Exercise 9.2. Review the link mnemonic that you have created for the passage on W. C. Fields. Then wait an hour or two and try to write down as much of its content as you can remember.

Using the cue-word mnemonic on longer passages

The paragraphs about the bagpipe and about W. C. Fields were not very long. Usually, the prose materials that we try to remember are quite a bit longer. Often a college student has to write for an hour, or a speaker speak for an hour without notes. So, in this next example a longer passage will be organized, memorized, and recalled using the cue-word mnemonic.

ADVERTISING

We are surrounded by advertising to such an extent that we don't even notice much of it. And what we do notice we often do not remember. Yet, life in modern America has been greatly affected by advertising, and the advertising industry plays an important role in the nation's economy. Every year more than $200 is spent on advertising for every man, woman, and child in the country. Advertising is the main support of our mass media. It supports all commercial radio and television and pays for two-thirds of the cost of newspapers and magazines. Advertising techniques have drastically changed how we go about selecting our nation's president.

Advertising may be thought of as a form of mass communication to promote a product, such as a brand of soap; to promote a service, such as using the telephone; to promote a person, such as a political candidate; or to promote an idea, such as voting for a new school tax. Advertising tries to get you to do something that you may not otherwise do. These communications are paid for by an identifiable individual or organization and are usually nonpersonal. Typically, someone doesn't walk up to you to introduce themselves and talk to you about a new product. The communication takes place through some media. In order of importance the advertising media are the newspapers, television, direct mailing, radio, magazines, and outdoor billboards.

The leading advertisers sell products, not services, people, or ideas. The biggest spenders are food companies, followed by drugs and cosmetics, soaps and cleansers, automobiles, and then tobacco. In fact, twenty-five percent of the money taken in through the sale of drugs and cosmetics is respent in advertising.

Even early civilizations had advertising. In ancient Babylonia merchants hired barkers to shout their wares to passers-by. In ancient Egypt signboards were placed outside doors telling what goods were sold there. Also, criers were hired to announce the arrival of ships with new cargoes of merchandise. The criers of ancient Greece were selected for their ability to enunciate clearly in proper Greek. They were sometimes accompanied by musicians.

The invention of printing with moveable type revolutionized man's means of communication and thus revolutionized advertising. In 1477 the first printed advertisement announced the sale of prayer books. In 1625 the first newspaper advertisement appeared in London. In 1704 Benjamin Franklin made advertisements more readable by using large headlines and surrounding the advertisement with white space.

As advertising became more widespread, the business of advertising evolved. At first newsdealers accepted advertisements for any U. S. newspaper. Newsdealers were then replaced in this task by advertising agents, who bought newspaper space at a discount from newspapers and then resold it to advertisers. Volney B. Palmer started the first U. S. advertising agency in Philadelphia in 1841. In 1875, also in Philadelphia, N. W. Ayer & Son began to emphasize the services that they could provide to advertisers. They hired writers and artists and carried out complete advertising campaigns for clients. This company was the prototype of our modern advertising agency.

Many advertising agencies are made up of four departments: a research department, a creative department, a media department, and a production department. The name of each department indicates what it does. The research department gathers information that will help devise effective advertisements for a specific product. They find out something about the potential buyers of the product, such as their age, income, and occupation. They also find out why people buy that type of product. Do they think that it will make them look younger or feel better? The American psychologist John Watson did much to develop this type of advertising research in the 1920s. The research department also does media research. For example, they find out who watches television and at what time of the day. The media department decides where to place the advertisements. Should all the ads be newspaper ads, or should some be TV ads? This decision depends on the type of product, the potential buyer, and other factors. The creative department makes up the ad. They write the copy, that is, the printed message of the ad. They create the artwork, too. The production department supervises the production of the advertisement, whether the ad was made for radio, television, magazines, or some other form of advertising media.

The advertising agency makes much of its profit by commissions from the media. If an advertiser ends up paying $100,000 to buy newspaper space, the agency usually gets a fifteen percent or $15,000 commission back from the newspaper. Today there are about 6,000 advertising agencies in the United States.

Before trying to deal with the passage about advertising let's look over the following summary of steps used in the cue-word mnemonic.

1. Read the material carefully until you understand all of it. Try to form visual images that represent the content of some parts of the passage.
2. Create the cue words.
3. Use separation lines to divide subtopics whenever necessary.
4. Eliminate unimportant or redundant cue words.
5. Use substitution mnemonics on abstract words and numbers.
6. Use a peg-type mnemonic or the link mnemonic to organize the cue words.
7. Review the mnemonic images.

I came up with the following list of cue words when I read the passage for the first time.

$200
2/3
president
product, service, person, idea
newspapers, television, direct mailing, radio, magazines, billboards
food, drugs-cosmetics, soap-cleansers, automobiles, tobacco
25%

---

criers
signboards
printing press
1477 prayer book
1625 newspaper ad
1704 Benjamin Franklin, large type, white spaces

Palmer, 1841, Philadelphia, first agency
Ayer, 1875, Philadelphia, complete services
research department
media department
creative department
production department
15%
6,000

The next step is to go through and eliminate some cue words. What words should be eliminated? Well, (1) those that you think you will automatically remember at the right time, and (2) those that represent what you consider to be unimportant information or information that you do not wish to remember. In the list of cue words *crier* and *signboard* do not seem to represent information that I wish to include. The string of words starting with *Palmer* is also eliminated because I want to memorize only information about the first agency that offered complete services. The word *president* I think that I will automatically remember along with the words *Philadelphia* and *complete services* that go with the information about the Ayer company. I also think that I will automatically remember *cosmetics,* if I remember *drugs; cleansers* if I remember *soap;* and *white spaces* if I remember *large type.* The decisions you make here, of course, may be different.

The next task is to take the remaining cue words and use substitution mnemonics on any that represent abstract words or numbers. The words in parentheses represent the substitutions that I have made.

$200—(noses)

2/3—(67%—chalk)

product, service, person, idea—(prod:duck, surf:vise, person, eye: deer)

newspaper, television, mail, radio, magazine, billboards

food, drugs, soap, automobiles, tobacco

25%—(nail)

---

printing press

1477—(tire:cake) prayer book

1625—(dish:nail) newspaper ad

1704—(tack:sewer), Benjamin Franklin, large type

N. W. Ayer—(new, white air)

1875—(dove:coal)

research—(test tube)

media—(meteor)

creative—(artist)

production—(factory)

15%—(towel)

6,000—(shoes:sauce)

The information in this passage about advertising has been reduced to forty-four cue words or cue phrases, and this total can be divided up into three groups of six, four, and eight sequences of cue words. The first group represents general information about advertising, the second group its history, and the third group general information about advertising agencies.

There are a number of ways that these forty-four cue words could be memorized. In this example I will attach the first group of cue words to the peg words associated with the numbers 51 to 56, the second group of cue words with the peg words for the numbers 61 to 64, and the third set of cue words with the numbers 71 to 78. If you don't remember your peg words for the numbers 1 to 100, then review Chapter 5 and look at the peg words in the Appendix. Many people prefer to use their 100 loci (Chapter 3) rather than the 100 peg words. You might try to memorize the cue words using your loci.

The first group is made up of the sets of cue words *noses; chalk; prod:duck, surf:vise, person, eye:deer; newspaper, television, mail, radio, magazine, billboard; food, drugs, soap, automobiles, tobacco;* and *nail.* Try to make up images from the descriptions I have provided. Note each image for detail, color, and interaction. If you simply read the descriptions, you will not remember the cue words. Each of the following italicized words represents my peg word for the number used.

51—(noses) The *lady* has two noses on her face.

52—(chalk) A *lion* is chewing on a big piece of chalk.

53—(prod:duck, surf:vise, person, eye:deer)—A piece of the *loom* is a sharp wooden prod, that is, a pointed stick. The moving prod prods a duck into the ocean surf. Washed by the surf is a large vise. The vise has a person caught between its jaws. The person has large brown eyes like a deer's.

54—(newspaper, television, mail, radio, magazine, billboard) A fishing *lure* hooks a rolled up newspaper. The newspaper is smacked against a television set. The television set is dropped into a mailbox. The mailbox grows knobs and a speaker and turns into a radio. The radio falls but lands on a pile of magazines. A magazine is torn up and its pages are pasted on a billboard.

55—(food, drugs, soap, automobiles, tobacco) A *lily* is eaten for food. Sprinkled on this food are pills and drugs from a bottle. The drugs are picked up and rubbed into a soapy lather. The soap foams and bubbles until it covers an automobile. The automobile is filled with shredded tobacco.

56—(nail) A *leech* wraps itself around a nail.

Exercise 9.3. Go back and review the images linking the peg words and the cue words in this set.

Exercise 9.4 Write down the cue words in this set from memory starting with the peg word for 51, *lady*.

Exercise 9.5. Wherever necessary transform the cue words back into the original abstract words or into numbers.

Exercise 9.6. Write out that part of the passage on advertising covered by the twenty-one cue words in this first group. Use your own words, but use the cue words to supply you with specific information and prompts for other information not part of the cues.

The next set of cue words consists of *printing press; tire: cake, prayer book; dish:nail, newspaper ad; tack:sewer, Benjamin Franklin, large type.* The images that I have created for this set are the following:

61—(printing press) A *sheet* is wrapped around a printing press.

62—(tire:cake, prayer book) A *chain* is attached to a tire. The tire rolls over a chocolate cake. From inside the cake comes a prayer book.

63—(dish:nail, newspaper ad) A *gem* is glued to a dish. The dish has a nail pounded through it. A nail is used to cut out a newspaper ad.

64—(tack:sewer, Benjamin Franklin, large type) A *chair* has a tack on its seat. The tack is thrown into the sewer. The sewer is being cleaned by Benjamin Franklin. Benjamin Franklin is writing his name in large type.)

Exercise 9.7. Repeat Exercises 9.3 to 9.6 for the second set of peg words and cue words starting with the peg word for 61, *sheet*.

Here are descriptions of possible images for associating the peg words for 71 to 78 and the last set of cue words.

71—(new, white air) The *cot* has a large container of new, white air resting on it.

72—(dove:coal) A gold *coin* has an engraving of a dove on it. The dove is carrying a piece of coal in its beak.

73—(test tube) A *comb* is placed in a test tube.

74—(meteor) A *car* is demolished by a meteor.

75—(artist) A large chunk of *coal* is being sculpted by an artist.

76—(factory) A large *couch* is carried into a factory.

77—(towel) A *cake* is being baked in a towel.

78—(shoes:sauce) *Coffee* is poured into a pair of shoes. The shoes are placed in a bowl of tomatoe sauce.

Exercise 9.8. Repeat Exercises 9.3 to 9.6 for this third set of words starting with the peg word *cot*.

Exercise 9.9. Wait a few hours and then try to recall all the cue words for the advertising passage. If there are some words that you cannot recall, then review the mental images containing those words and try to make them more distinct.

*Exercise 9.10. Use the cue-word technique to memorize some of the information from the following passage on *Hypnosis*. After using one of the peg-word mnemonics or the method of loci to memorize the cue words, review the mnemonic images at least once before you try to recall the passage. If you feel that you are having difficulty remembering many cue words, limit your final list of cue words to about twelve cues organized into two sets of about six cue words each. You don't have to remember *everything* in the passage.

HYPNOSIS

There are more than 100 definitions of hypnosis, but nobody really knows what it is. There is no set of measures that can be used to tell us whether someone is in a hypnotic trance or not. Hypnosis is often compared to being asleep. This is partly because of the way hypnosis is induced. The person being hypnotized, the hypnotic subject, may be asked by the hypnotist to fix his gaze on something. The subject is then told that he is getting tired and should close his eyes and relax. The subject's breathing may become deep and regular just as if he were asleep. However, hypnosis is not sleep in the usual sense of the word. The hypnotized person hears what the hypnotist says and can act and move as would a person awake. His behavior does seem strange, though. He seems to do automatically what the hypnotist tells him. The hypnotic trance seems to be more like the state of a sleep walker.

The existence of trance-like states can be found in the recorded history of many different cultures, but the modern discovery of hypnosis has generally been credited to Franz Anton Mesmer who in the 1770s in France found that ill people benefitted when he touched them. Mesmer believed that he was gifted with animal magnetism which he could transfer to sick people and heal them. Thus, hypnotism was first known as *mesmerism*. However, a commission sponsored by the French government which included that eminent American, Benjamin Franklin, reported in 1784 that *magnetism* had nothing to do with the effects created by Mesmer. The effects were the result of people's *imaginations*.

In the 1840s James Braid labeled the phenomenon *hypnotism* from the Greek word *hypnos* meaning *sleep*. Medical doctors began to use hypnosis in surgery before the time that anesthetic drugs became available. Around 1900 Freud used hypnosis in his treatment of neurotic disorders. By hypnotizing his patients he found that they could recall emotionally disturbing personal events that they otherwise couldn't remember. Although hypnosis has been used for quite a long time, systematic scientific research on hypnosis has occurred only recently. As a result of his investigations, Clark Hull in 1933 suggested that hypnosis is a state of *hypersuggestability* in which the hypnotized subject responds to the suggestions of the hypnotist to the greatest extent possible.

Hypnosis has captured the interest of many people because it suggests complete control of one person by another. The hypnotized person seems to do things suggested by the hypnotist that he otherwise wouldn't do. For example, an illusory experience can be induced in which the subject will enjoy eating a raw onion if he is told that it is an apple. Hallucinations can be induced in which the subject seems to perceive and talk to a person who is not physically present. The hypnotized subject will also demonstrate age regression in which he re-experiences events that occurred in his childhood and will talk, act, and write as he did at that age. Some of the most impressive results of hypnosis have to do with the suppression of pain. After being given the appropriate suggestion, some hypnotized subjects can have their skins pierced by needles or have their hands placed in icy water with no show of discomfort. When asked what they are experiencing, they say they feel no pain. This hypnotic anesthesia has been of benefit in a number of areas of medical treatment.

Post-hypnotic suggestion is another interesting aspect of hypnosis. The hypnotist can request the subject to later perform acts while out of the hypnotic trance, and the hypnotized subject will perform these acts and not be aware of the reason. For example, the hypnotist may tell the person that when he hears the word *dog*, he will see water rising in the room. When the hypnotist says the word *dog*, the person, who is no longer hypnotized, will jump on a chair and look very distressed.

In spite of these convincing demonstrations of hypnotic suggestion, recent research has shown that much of the behavior of hypnotized subjects can be elicited from subjects who are asked only to pretend that they are hypnotized. These subjects are called *simulators,* and the behavior of these simulators often cannot be distinguished even by experts from the behavior of hypnotized subjects. But there are still some behaviors induced by hypnosis that are very difficult to simulate. These include hallucinations and suppression of pain. Also, simulators do not seem able to forget events the way hypnotized subjects do; nor can they later perform actions under post-hypnotic suggestion and be unaware of the reason for their behavior. One should keep in mind, however, that hallucination and anesthesia in hypnosis can be induced in only about ten percent of the general population. Nevertheless, the effects of hypnosis can be both strong and long lasting. Because of this a hypnotist needs special training not only in hypnotic techniques but in related areas of medicine and psychology.

Hypnosis seems to be primarily a motivational effect. Hypnotized subjects try to do what is suggested to them by the hypnotist, but they will not perform any act that they consider morally or legally wrong and that they would not do in their normal non-hypnotic state. Hypnosis will not increase physical strength or athletic performance any more than any other motivating technique. In fact, hypnosis can result in an athlete pushing himself to the point that physical injury occurs. Unfortunately, hypnosis doesn't seem to enhance the learning of new information or the recall of information previously learned in a non-hypnotic state. If motivated to do his or her best, the same degree of learning and remembering can occur in a non-hypnotized person. Often the hypnotized person who seems to be remembering some past event in great detail is really elaborating and fabricating much of the information, but is convinced that the events being described actually occurred. This seems to be what is taking place when hypnotized subjects are asked to describe their previous lives. Whether hypnosis can increase artistic or scientific creativity is not known.

chapter ten

Conclusion

Some of you who have worked through the nine previous chapters will feel comfortable in using all the mnemonics that have been discussed and will use them effectively. To you I offer my congratulations. However, most of you will feel at ease with some of the techniques, somewhat at ease with others, but feel fairly inept with the more difficult procedures such as the face-name mnemonic and the cue-word mnemonic. To you I say, "Don't give up." Some of the mnemonics that have been described are very difficult because they are based on a number of different steps and draw upon a variety of more basic skills. These involve the ability to form effective visual images and use a variety of encoding techniques. The more you use these mnemonics the better you get implementing them. Using mnemonic devices effectively is a skill that can be learned. As with most skills, some people learn faster and better than others, but all of us get better with practice.

You may find that a difficult mnemonic, such as the cue-word mnemonic of Chapter 9 is not working for you at all; that is, you can recall very little using the menmonic cues. If this does occur, try to use it and practice with it anyway. The cue-word mnemonic, as all mnemonics, is a plan for memorizing, and unless you believe you have some better plan, then you shouldn't give it up. A mnemonic such as the cue-word mnemonic forces you to interact with the material that you want to remember. It provides you with a series of specific steps that allow you to comprehend, review, and memorize information. You will certainly learn something using the mnemonic even if you don't use it to recall. For example, after using the cue-word mnemonic to memorize the contents of a prose passage, you probably will be able to remember a great deal about the passage even if you do not try to recall it using the mnemonic cues. However, you should reach the point where you can do *better* recalling if you use the mnemonic cues rather than simply trying to remember the passage. Utilizing a mnemonic that you still feel uncomfortable with is certainly better than staring at something that you know you should be trying to memorize and saying to yourself over and over, "Oh, I know that I will *never* be able to remember all that." Use a mnemonic: it's a plan, a blueprint, a recipe. Remember, you get better at it with practice.

In the previous nine chapters I have presented the basic mnemonic procedures; these procedures seem to be the most useful and provide a foundation for using other mnemonic devices. There are many other mnemonic techniques, and you may want to look at the books listed in the Bibliography to learn more about them. However, these other techniques are based on the same mnemonic skills that have been discussed here. The more adept you become with one mnemonic, the easier it should be to learn to use others.

Appendix

10. toes, dice, autos, daisy, yachts, weights, woods, thighs
11. tot, tooth, daddy, tattoo, toad, tide, dude, tweed, Teddy, Edith
12. tin, twine, dean, dawn, ton, tan, tune, twin, town, Tony, Edna, Diana
13. tomb, team, dam, atom, dome, dame, thumb, dummy, dime, Tommy, Adam
14. tire, deer, tower, tray, heater, water, waiter, author, Dora, Audrey
15. towel, doll, outlaw, tool, tile, dial, hotel, tail, idol, Dolly, Ethel
16. dish, ditch, tissue, Dutch
17. tack, dog, duck, attic, duke, toga, dock, deck, Dick
18. dove, taffy, dive, thief, Dave, TV
19. tub, tape, tuba, dope, tap, adobe, tepee, depot
20. nose, noise, noose, knees, niece, news, Hans, hyenas
21. net, aunt, window, nut, knight, knot, ant, hand, hound, nightie, Annette
22. nun, onion, union, noon, Nan, Nina
23. gnome, name, enemy, numb
24. wiener, winner, owner, narrow, Nora, Henry, Nero
25. nail, knoll, kneel, Nile, Noel, Nellie
26. notch, hinge, winch, inch
27. neck, ink, hankie, wink, Hank, Nick, eunuch, yankee, nag
28. knife, nephew, navy
29. knob, nap
30. moose, mouse, hymns, hams, mess, mace, moss, maze, Amos
31. mat, mud, mouth, meat, maid, meadow, moth, moat, mutt, Maud, Matthew
32. moon, money, minnow, man, woman, ammonia, mane, mine, Minnie, Mona
33. mummy, mama, memo, Mimi, Mamie
34. mower, hammer, mayor, amour, mare, Mary, Myra, Murray, mire
35. mule, mill, mail, mole, meal, Mollie, Emily
36. match, mesh, mush
37. mug, hammock, mike, Mike, Maggie, Mac
38. movie, muff, Mafia
39. mop, map, mob, hump, imp, hemp
40. rose, warehouse, horse, race, heroes, rice, oars, hairs, heiress, Rosie, Horace

41. rod, wart, root, radio, road, rat, heart, art, Howard, Ruth, Rita, Harriet, yard, rut
42. horn, rain, iron, rhino, urn, arena, yarn, rein, wren, Irene, Aaron, Irwin, Warren
43. ram, arm, harem, rum, room, rim, army, worm, Irma
44. rower, rear, warrior, error
45. rail, railway, roll, reel, earl, Earle, Errol
46. roach, rouge, arch, ridge, rash, rajah, Archie
47. rock, rug, rag, rake, wreck, Eric, ark, arc, rook, rookie, rogue, rig
48. roof, reef, wharf, Harvey
49. rope, harp, robe, herb, rabbi, wrap, orb, rip, Arab, Herb, Rob
50. lace, lasso, wheels, Alice, Lewis, Lucy, Elsie, Louise, alleys, willows, alehouse
51. lady, lad, lid, lead, wallet, loot, light, load, lute, Hilda, Lottie, Lloyd, Eliot
52. lion, lawn, alien, lane, Alan, Helen, Ellen, Leon, Halloween
53. loom, lamb, lime, limb, elm, helium, William
54. lure, lawyer, healer, lyre, liar, Larry, Laura, Leroy
55. lily, Lily, Lola, Lulu, Lowell, Lyle
56. ledge, leech, latch, lodge, leash, eyelash
57. log, lake, leg, lock, elk, Olga, Alec, Luke
58. lava, wolf, olive, leaf, love, elf, laugh
59. lip, lap, lobby, elbow, loop
60. cheese, chess, juice, jaws, shows, watches, Jessie, Jess
61. sheet, jet, chute, hatchet, shed, shadow, jade, Judy
62. chain, gin, chin, ocean, genii, Jonah, June, John, Jenny, Jane, Eugene, Gene, Jean
63. gem, chum, jam, gym, Jim
64. chair, cherry, jury, jar, shore, sherry, shower, usher, washer, Jerry
65. jello, jelly, jewel, jail, shawl, shell, cello, Shelley, Julia, Jill, Joel
66. choo-choo, judge, Joshua
67. chalk, cheek, shack, sheik, jug, chick, jockey, Jackie, Jake
68. chef, chief, Jeff
69. ship, sheep, shop, chop, chip, chap
70. case, gas, wax, gauze, goose, kiss, ox, ax, Gus
71. cot, cat, coat, kit, goat, kid, gut, caddy, kite, God, Keith, Kate

72. coin, queen, wagon, cane, can, gown, canoe, acne, Connie, Ken, Gwynne
73. comb, wigwam, game, Kim
74. car, crow, gear, crew, choir, core, Gary, Carrie
75. coal, glue, eagle, igloo, clay, claw, keyhole, coolie, Kelly, Clay
76. couch, coach, gage, cage
77. cake, coke, cook, cookie, cuckoo, keg, quake
78. coffee, cave, cuff, calf, cafe
79. cup, cowboy, cape, cab, cap, cob, cube
80. vase, fuse, face, vise, office, fez, fuzz, waves
81. foot, photo, vat, food, fat, voodoo
82. fan, phone, fin, oven, vine, Van, Ivan, Fannie, Yvonne
83. foam, fume, fame
84. fur, fire, ivory, wafer, weaver, fir, fairy, ferry, Vera
85. file, fly, valley, fool, fellow, veil, waffle, fuel, veal, viola, Phil, Flo
86. fish, fudge
87. fig, fog, folk, fag, Vic
88. fife, five, Fifi
89. fob, VIP, fop, Phoebe
90. bus, boss, bass, base, piece, booze, posse, peas, Bessie
91. bat, bed, boat, pot, poet, boot, beet, bath, bead, booth, body, Patti, Betty, Buddy, Pete, Pat
92. bone, pan, pen, pin, penny, pine, weapon, piano, pony, bean, ebony, pane, Bonnie, Ben
93. bum, bomb, palm, beam
94. bear, beer, pear, berry, opera, pier, burro, bureau, bower, bar, Perry
95. bell, ball, apple, pail, pillow, bowl, belly, pool, plow, bale, pulley, Bill, Belle, Paul, Paula, Polly, Billie
96. badge, beach, pouch, bush, peach, page, patch, beech
97. book, bag, pig, pack, pick, bug, buck, back, Becky, Peggy
98. beef, puff
99. pipe, baby, papa, pup, pope, pub, Bobby
100. disease, theses, Odysseus, daisies, deuces, outhouses

POSSIBLE PEG WORDS FOR THE NUMBERS 0 TO 09:

0. hose, eyes, ice, house, zoo, ace, saw, sow, Sue
00. sauce, seas, seesaw, saws, houses, zoos, sows, icehouse, Susie, Zeus
01. soda, city, seat, waist, soot, seed, stew, seaweed, acid, suit, sod, Sid, Sadie
02. swan, sun, swine, son, sign, snow
03. seam, psalm, swim, Sam, Sammie, zoom
04. sewer, czar, Sarah, hawser, hussar, seer, hosiery
05. sleigh, whistle, weasel, cell, soil, seal, easel, sail, Sallie, Hazel, Celia
06. sash, switch, sage, sewage
07. ski, whiskey, sock, sack, sky, squaw, hassock, Isaac, Zeke
08. safe, sofa, salve, sieve, Sophie
09. soup, soap, spy, wasp, subway, sub

Example solutions
for selected exercises

Exercise 2.2.

(tree/hammer)—Think of a tree having its leaves knocked down by being battered with a giant hammer.

(ship/piano)—A ship is carrying a large piano that is rolling around on the deck.

(fork/barrel)—A fork is stuck into the side of a wooden barrel.

(arrow/newspaper)—An arrow pierces a man's newspaper and fastens it against the wall.

(flag/door)—A flag is carried into a building but gets stuck in the revolving door.

(umbrella/church)—An umbrella is blown onto the steeple of a church.

(chair/toast)—A chair has a stack of toast placed on it.

(volcano/harp)—A volcano erupts and a harp shoots out of its top.

(trumpet/flower)—A pretty song is played by a trumpet and flowers grow out of its bell.

(bottle/shoes)—A retired shoemaker builds small model shoes in bottles.

Exercise 2.4.

(hardware store counter/glue)—Glue is being smeared all over the counter.

(glue/tacks)—Tacks are being scattered on the wet glue.

(tacks/steel wire)—Tacks are used to attach the end of a steel wire to the floor.

(steel wire/hacksaw)—The steel wire is cut in two by the hacksaw.

(hacksaw/can of red paint)—The hacksaw is painted with red paint.

(red paint/copper tubing)—The red paint is poured through some copper tubing.

(copper tubing/lubricating oil)—From the end of the copper tubing drips lubricating oil.

(lubricating oil/yardstick)—The oil runs down the length of the yardstick.

(yardstick/file)—The wooden yardstick is filed smooth with a file.

(file/small hammer)—The file is struck with a hammer and makes a ringing sound.

Exercise 2.6.

(Charlie Chaplin/auto)—Charlie Chaplin is driving an auto.

(auto/tramp)—An auto runs over a poor tramp.

(tramp/floor)—A tramp slips and falls down on a slippery floor.

(floor/pawn shop)—The floor of a pawn shop cracks and all the merchandise falls into the basement.

(pawn shop/immigrant)—The pawn shop is rebuilt by an immigrant in foreign clothing.

(immigrant/arms)—The immigrant has three arms.

(arms/kid)—Two arms are holding a kid.

(kid/gold)—The kid is playing with a gold nugget.

(gold/city)—A gold nugget is thrown at the city hall.

(city/dictator)—The city hall is being demolished by the dictator.

Exercise 2.7.

The soldier wore a *linen* uniform and a *helmet.* His *captain* told him to go into the *school* and find some *fruit.* When he entered, the soldier saw a *rocket* in the *cellar.* It was lying in a *cradle,* and next to it was a *teacher* who held a *needle* and was ready to use it to fire the rocket. The rocket was aimed at the *beach* and the teacher held a *Bible.*

Exercise 4.1.

1. panorama—*pan:ram; piano:ram, pan:oar:(ram:ma)*
2. tradition—*tray:dish; tray:dish:(onion)*
3. Collier—*collie:ear*
4. mutiny—*moon:tin:(knee)*
5. danger—*den:jar*
6. Flanagan—*flannel:gown; flame:gun*
7. mortgage—*mare:tea:(gage); mark:kids*
8. role—*roll*
9. commercial—*comet:shell; camera:shell; camel:shell*
10. Weintraub—*wine:tub; vine:tribe*
11. ambition—*yam:mission; yam:bit:(shin)*
12. social—*soap:shell; soup:shell*
13. Tuttle—*turtle*
14. stare—*stair*
15. owner—*oaf:nurse*
16. wrath—*raft; wreath*
17. Lawrence—*lure:wrench; log:wench*
18. shriek—*shiek; sherry:key*
19. donor—*doughnut; dome:oar; dune:ore*
20. Washington—*wash:ring:(thumb)*
21. verb—*herb; fur:bee*
22. pollution—*pole:lotion; pole:lute:(skin)*
23. Applebaum—*apple:bomb*
24. labor—*leg:boar; lake:oar; lab:ore*

25. victory—*wick:story; wick:story:(eel)*
26. cowardice—*cow:wart:(dice); cow:art:ice*

Exercise 4.2.

1. term—*termite; terminal*
2. knowledge—*knoll:ledge; Nile:lodge*
3. ceremony—*cellar:money; serum:knee; Sarah:money*
4. Knapp—*knapsack; nap*
5. device—*devil:ice; deer:vise*
6. retreat—*wheat:treat; weed:feet*
7. Bradley—*braid:leaf; brat:leak*
8. despair—*dish:pear; disc:spear*
9. democracy—*demon:rock:(sea)*
10. meeting—*meat:ink*

Exercise 5.1.

1. 65
2. 0
3. 1214
4. 120
5. 5
6. 646
7. 372
8. 21
9. 53
10. 781
11. 9514
12. 28
13. 7425
14. 9071
15. 97
16. 647
17. 851
18. 746

19. 017
20. 048

Exercise 5.2.

For possible encodings of items 1, 2, 3, 4, 5, 7, 8, 10, 11, 12, 14, 15, 17, 18, and 20, see the Appendix. The other list items are encoded as follows:

6. 309 can be coded as *mishap* or *misplay*, neither of which is high in imagery. It is better to break 309 into 3:09 or 30:9.

9. 691 can be coded as chapped, Egypt, chopped, shaped, chipped, jabbed. It is better to break 691 into 6:91 or 69:1.

13. 007 can be coded into seasick.

16. 083 doesn't seem to be codable unless it is broken into 0:83 or 08:3.

19. 277 can be coded into Hancock. It is better to break 277 into 2:77 or 27:7.

Exercise 5.8.

1. shirt/$11.19—*tot:tub*—The shirt was taken off the tot. The tot was then put in a tub.

2. paint/$7.45—*cow:rail*—Paint is poured over a cow. The cow is standing on a railroad track.

3. sofa/$575.00—*owl:coal*—On the sofa is standing an owl. The owl has a piece of coal in its beak.

4. skillet/$6.31—*witch:mat*—The skillet is held by a witch. The witch is wiping her foot on a doormat.

5. cannon/$1549.79—*towel:rope:cup*—A cannon is covered with a towel. On one end of the towel is tied a rope. The other end of the rope is tied to a cup.

6. crown/$8750.90—*fig:lace:bus*—A valuable crown has a fig stuck on it. The fig is wrapped in a piece of lace. The lace is run over by a bus.

7. bouquet/$4.96—*arrow:badge*—A bouquet of flowers has an arrow stuck in it. On the arrow is pinned a policeman's badge.

8. hatchet/$6.29—*witch:knob*—A hatchet chops a witch in half. From inside the witch falls a doorknob.

9. spear/$21.10—*net:toes*—A spear is thrown and caught in a net. The heavy net falls on your toes.

10. globe/$25.65—*nail:jello*—A globe has a big nail sticking out of it. On the head of the nail is a gob of jello.

Exercise 5.9.

1. garden shovel/39—*mop*—A shovel has a mop on the other end of its handle.
2. metal barrel/75—*coal*—Imagine a metal barrel full of coal.
3. steel chain/Z11—*zebra:tot*—Think of a steel chain tied to a zebra's neck with a tot holding the other end as a leash.
4. electric drill/12M—*tin:emperor*—An electric drill is drilling through a sheet of tin. The sheet of tin contains a picture of Napoleon.
5. window fan/X64S—*ax:chair:eskimo*—A window fan is being smashed by an ax. The ax hits a chair. The chair has an Eskimo sitting in it.
6. small rowboat/AK113—*ape:cane:tie:tomb*—A small rowboat contains an ape. The ape is paddling with a cane. The cane has a bow tie tied to it. The bow tie flies off and lands on a tomb.
7. fishhooks/4157B—*rod:log:beet*—Fishhooks are tied to a fishing rod. The fishing rod is resting on a log. On the log some beets are being chopped up.
8. pencil sharpener/P80—*pea:vase*—A pencil sharpener is sharpening a pea. The pea is placed in a vase.

Exercise 6.2.

For some of the historic dates two alternative example solutions are given. In the second solution the first two digits of the date are not used. Also, the cue word from the event is used without being transformed into a keyword.

cue word—(keyword)—*encoded numbers*—Description of the images formed.

1. Armada—(arm)—*towel:fife*—An arm is holding up a bath towel. Wrapped inside the towel is a fife.
2. Bible—(Bible)—*dish:tot*—Resting on a Bible is a dish. The dish is being tipped over by a tot.
3. plague—(plague)—*dish:jello*—Some bacteria from the plague has been placed in a dish. They are eating jello.

4. Philadelphia—(Phil)—*dish:fan*—Phil picks up a dish. The dish falls on a fan.

5a. massacre—(massacre)—*tack:case*—A massacre takes place when thousands of tacks are shot into a crowd. All the tacks are then picked up and put into a suitcase.

5b. massacre—*case*—At the Boston Massacre the British used a case of bullets.

6a. Alamo—(Al:ammo)—*taffy:match*—Al is running out of ammo. The ammo is made out of taffy. The taffy is lit with a match.

6b. Alamo—*match*—At the Alamo the Mexicans lit a match.

7a. Gettysburg—(ghetto)—*thief:gem*—Into the ghetto ran the thief. He was carrying a gem.

7b. Gettysburg—*gem*—Gettysburg heard a gem of a speech.

8a. Suez Canal—(sewer)—*TV:ship*—In the sewer floated the TV. The TV was hit by a ship.

8b. Suez Canal—*ship*—The Suez Canal was used by the ship.

9a. Prohibition—(Pro)—*tuba:attic*—The Pro played the tuba. The tuba was stored in the attic.

9b. Prohibition—*attic*—Prohibition forced the man to drink in his attic.

10a. chancellor—(cellar)—*tape:mummy*—The cellar was full of tape. The tape was used to wrap a mummy.

10b. chancellor—*mummy*—Hitler as chancellor was as scary as a mummy.

Exercise 6.3.

In the answers given here both the last name and the telephone number were associated using the link mnemonic with the keyword derived from the first name. You may have made a keyword using only the last name. Also, the digits are grouped into a 2-1-2-2 pattern. Your pattern may be different.

1. Oscar Knapp—(car:knapsack)—*jello:owl:mug:cot*—In the car was a knapsack. The knapsack contained jello. The jello was being eaten by an owl. The owl lifted a beer mug. The mug fell onto a cot.

2. Conrad Levinson—(con:leaf)—*ski:Ma:lady:vase*—The con wore nothing but a leaf. The leaf was shaped like a ski. The ski fell on top of Ma. Ma bumped into a lady. The lady was carrying a vase.

3. Calvin Collier—(vine:collie)—*dove:hose:log:ski*—A vine was being

chewed on by a collie. The collie was then pecked by a dove. The dove was squirted by a hose. A log fell on the hose and broke it. The log was made into a pair of skis.

4. Beatrice   Flanagan—(beet:flannel:gown)—*cheese:arrow:bus:fife*—A red beet stained a flannel gown. The gown was then used to wrap up cheese. The cheese was struck by an arrow. The arrow was placed on a bus. The bus ran over and squashed a fife.

5. Monica   Friedlander—(harmonica:freezer)—*nail:arrow:mop:lady*—A harmonica was put into a freezer. The freezer was sealed with a nail. The nail was used as the point of an arrow. The arrow was shot into a mop. The mop was swung by a lady.

6. Ethel Applebaum—(hill:apple)—*mat:hose:roof:movie*—On top of the hill was a giant apple. The apple rested on a mat. The mat was sprayed by a hose. The hose leaked onto the roof. On the roof was being shown a movie.

7. Sydney Bradley—(knee:braid)—*sauce:cow:horn:bat*—On my knee was a girl's braid. The braid had been dipped in taco sauce. The sauce was being licked by a cow. The cow blew a horn. The horn was dented by a baseball bat.

8. Deborah Jasper—(boar:spear)—*moose:hose:tin:coal*—A boar was hit by a spear. The spear was caught by a moose. The moose became entangled in a hose. The hose knocked over a tin can. The can was filled with coal.

9. Ashley Saccoccia—(ash:sack:coach)—*mummy:witch:lion:roof*—The wood ash was placed into a sack. The sack was loaded into a stagecoach. Inside the stagecoach was a mummy. The mummy was dancing with a witch. The witch was petting a lion. The lion climbed onto the roof.

10. Flora Reynolds—(floor:wren)—*cup:Ma:coal:chain*—On the floor landed a wren. The wren started to drink out of a cup. The cup was kicked over by Ma. Ma worked mining coal. The coal was raised by a chain.

Exercise 6.4.

word—(pronunciation)—definition—*keyword*—mnemonic sentence

1. implacable—(im-PLAY-ka-bull)—not of a nature to be calmed or pacified—*play:bull*—If you play with a bull, it will not calm down.

2. fetish—(FEE—tish)—primitive magic charm—*feet:itch*—My feet itch, but my fetish will cure them.

3. gullible—(GULL-a-bull)—easily tricked—*gull*—The gull was tricked out of its money.

4. rancor—(RANG-cur)—strong ill will—*cur*—I would like to shoot that cur (inferior dog).

5. hegemony—(he-GEM-oh-knee)—one nation ruling over other nations—*gem*—The nation with all the gems controls the others.

6. magnate—(MAG-nate)—a person prominent in industry management—*magnet*—He ran the industry with a magnetic personality.

7. tacit—(TASS-it)—silent consent—*tassle*—The man with the tassle on his hat silently consented.

8. adipose—(AD-a-pose)—fat stored in the connective tissue of the body—*ad:pose*—The ad contained a fat man posing.

9. extirpate—(EK-stir-pate)—to pull out by the roots—*stir*—He stirred the dirt around and pulled out the root.

10. ignominy—(ig-NO-minnie)—disgrace; conduct deserving disgrace—*nominee*—The nominee is not here because his conduct was disgraceful.

11. harbinger—(HAR-bin-jer)—a forerunner, a sign—*binge*—Uncle Oscar's three-day binge was a sign of worse to come.

12. jejune—(gee-JUNE)—not of interest or satisfaction; insipid—*Gee June*—Gee, June is not a very interesting person.

Exercise 6.5.

1. marriage(age)—*I aged* after my marr*iage*.

2. among(mongrel)—He is a *mong*rel a*mong* dogs.

3. weird(we)—*We* are *we*ird b*ird*s.

4. tragedy(age)—This is an *age* of tr*age*dy.

5. despair(pair)—Here are a *pair* of *des*ks.

6. shepherd(herd)—The shep*herd* watched a *herd* of goats.

7. parallel(all)—*All* the lines must be par*alle*l.

8. dealt(deal)—I was *deal*t a bad *deal*.

9. nickel(element)—Nick*el* is an *el*ement.

10. seize(seaport)—The pirates *sei*zed the *sea*port.

Exercise 7.1.

Washington Always Journeyed Many Miles And Jumped Village Hedges.

The problem with this list is that you have to remember that John Adams came before John Quincy Adams, Jefferson came before Jackson, and Madison before Monroe.

Exercise 7.3.

For the first letter solution let's try to use a *poetic* sentence, since we are trying to memorize a list of poets. I devised,

"Beautiful Books Will Contain Sweet But Simple Kindness."

To memorize this list using a peg-word mnemonic, I used the peg words representing the numbers 91 to 98.

91. bat—The bat suffered some painful burns (Burns).
92. bone—The bone splashed into the lake (Blake).
93. bum—The bum was spouting long words (Wordsworth).
94. bear—The bear was carrying a basket of coal (Coleridge).
95. bell—The bell was rung by the Scot (Scott).
96. badge—The badge was worn by the baron (Byron).
97. book—The book fell on the delicate shell (Shelley).
98. beef—The beef contained an old key (Keats).

Exercise 7.4.

Using the first-letter mnemonic my sentence is "Leonardo Must Reach Greatness To Correctly Draw Her." As an alternative, the first syllable of each name was replaced by a high-imagery substitute word and the link mnemonic was used to chain together the substitute words. The following sentences describe the images formed. The italicized words are the substitute words.

The *lion* roared into the *mike*. The *mike* was hit by the *raft*. The *raft* broke the *jar*. In the *jar* was some *tissue*. Wrapped in the *tissue* was an apple *core*. The apple *core* was glued to the *door*. The *door* was used to cover the *hole*.

If you had to use more than one substitute word to encode each name, such as Lion:oar:dough, Mike:angel, Raft:eel, Jar:Joe:knee, Door:ear, and Hole:pine, then it is better to use a peg-word menomonic and associate each string with a separate peg word.

Exercise 8.3.

1. Webb—*web*
2. Malone—*melon, balloon*
3. Flanagan—*flannel:gown, flame:gun*
4. Pincelli—*pin:jelly*
5. Riedel—*rye:doll*
6. Tuttle—*turtle*
7. Fraser—*freezer, razor*
8. Collier—*collie:ear*
9. Gibson—*jeep:sun, gag:son*
10. Pinkham—*pink:ham, pin:can*
11. Sayre—*saw:oar, sailor*
12. Lawrence—*log:wrench, lure:wrench*

Exercise 8.4.

Listed for each of the names and photographs are the following: (1) a possible encoding of the last name, (2) a distinctive feature of the face, and (3) a suggested image for linking (1) and (2).

Name—(encoding of name), distinctive facial feature—Description of image for associating name and feature.

1. Debra Smelter—(smelter), very pale skin—Image this person working by a glowing furnace with her face lighted up by the fire.

2. Mike Vest—(vest), very broad smile—Image this person wearing a vest around his face, and when he smiles the vest opens popping all its buttons.

3. Kathy Spangler—(spangles), curly black hair—Image this person's hair being brushed back and covered with many small, shiny spangles.

4. Keith Rothman—(rock:man), high forehead—Image this high forehead being covered with marble rock by a man.

5. Gloria Philpot—(filled pot), dark eyes and eye sockets—Image the two eye sockets being filled with dark liquid from a pot.

6. Vernon Birteker—(bird:acre), strip of metal across top of glasses—Image a bird sitting on the horizontal strip of metal. The bird then flies into an acre of wheat.

7. Brian Wolfe—(Wolf), heavy eyebrows—Image a wolf with a furry face and heavy eyebrows.

8. Lotta Fischerstrom—(fisher:stream), round frames for glasses—Image a fisherman using the round parts of the frames as fishing reels. The fisher is, of course, fishing in a stream.

Exercise 9.1.

The first set of cue words that I generated was the following: 1879, Claude William Dunkenfield, 1946, juggler, 1939. *You Can't Cheat an Honest Man,* 1940, *My Little Chickadee,* 1941, *Never Give a Sucker an Even Break,* wit, coward, anti-establishment, drunken misfit. However, 1879 could be reduced to 79. I thought that if I could remember Dunkenfield, then I would remember Claude William. 1946 could be reduced to 46. The three movies were made in 1939, 1940, and 1941, so if I could remember 39, I would remember the three years. The names of each movie could be reduced to one cue word resulting in Cheat, Chickadee, and Sucker. The cue words are listed with their encodings as follows:

W. C. Fields
79/cup
Philadelphia/Phil
Dunkenfield/donkey:field

46/roach
juggler
39/mop
cheat/cheek
chickadee
sucker
wit/whip
coward/cow:herd
anti-establishment/aunt:eye
drunk

If you have memorized the 100 peg words, then you should automatically recognize your peg words for 79 (cup), 46 (roach), and 39 (mop). I have described the images I formed as follows:

(W. C. Fields/cup)—Think of Fields drinking from a cup.

(cup/Phil)—Inside the cup swims my friend Phil.

(Phil/donkey:field)—Phil leaps onto the back of a donkey standing in a field.

(donkey:field/roach)—The donkey on the field is chasing a roach.

(roach/juggler)—The roach is stepped on by a juggler.

(juggler/mop)—The juggler is juggling a mop.

(mop/cheek)—The mop is then balanced on his cheek.

(cheek/chickadee)—The cheek has a chickadee inside it.

(chickadee/sucker)—The chickadee is eating a sucker.

(sucker/whip)—The sucker is hit by a whip.

(whip/cow:herd)—The whip is trampled by a herd of cows.

(cow:herd/aunt:eye)—The herd of cows was frightened by my auntie's eye.

(aunt:eye/drunk)—My auntie's eye also frightened the drunk.

Exercise 9.10.

The following list consists of the cue words that I came up with:

sleep
hear
move

Franz Anton Mesmer
1770s
magnetism
Franklin
1784
imagination
1840s
James Braid
anesthetic
1900
Freud
Clark Hull
1933
hypersuggestability

---

illusion
onion
hallucination
age regression
pain
post-hypnotic suggestion
water

---

simulators
10%
training

---

motivation
legally wrong
athlete
learning
previous lives

Rather than using all of these cue words, I chose twelve; one set of five (sleep, Mesmer, 1840s, Braid, Freud) and one set of seven (illusion, hallucination, age regression, pain, post-hypnotic suggestion, simulators, motivation). The cue words are listed with their encodings as follows:

sleep/sleeve
Mesmer/mermaid
40s/roses
Braid/braid
Freud/frog

---

illusion/eel:loop:(chin)
hallucination/hall:shoe:(Asian)
age regression/reed:dress:(shin)
pain/pan
post-hypnotic suggestion/post
simulators/sink:mule:(lake)
motivation/motor:station

To memorize the first five cue words I used the peg words for the numbers 31 to 35. To memorize the next seven cue words I used the peg words for the numbers 41 to 47. Each italicized word represents my peg word for the number used.

31—(sleeve) A welcome *mat* was being used to wipe off a sleeve.

32—(mermaid) The *moon* had a figure of a mermaid on it.

33—(roses) The *mummy* was carrying a bouquet of roses.

34—(braid) A lawn *mower* was being used to cut off the girl's braid.

35—(frog) A *mule* was kicking a frog.

41—(eel:loop) A fishing *rod* was used to catch an eel. The eel formed itself into a giant loop.

42—(hall:shoe) The *horn* was blown loudly in the hall. The hall was filled with shoes.

43—(reed:dress) The *ram* was running through the reeds. The reeds were being woven into a beautiful dress.

44—(pan) The *rower* was rowing a large frying pan.

45—(post) A railroad *rail* was pounded into the ground as a post.

46—(sink:mule) A *roach* was running around in the sink. He was eaten by the mule.

47—(motor:station) A large *rock* was dropped on the motor. It had to be taken to the gas station.

Bibliography

General

The following listed books and articles describe the various mnemonics techniques and how to use them effectively.

Bower, G.H., Analysis of a mnemonic device. *American Scientist,* 1970, *58*, 496-510.

Brothers, J.D., & Eagen, E.P.F. *10 days to a successful memory.* Englewood Cliffs, N.J.: Prentice-Hall, 1957.

Cermak, L.S. *Improving your memory.* New York: McGraw-Hill, 1975.

Furst, B. *Stop forgetting.* (L. Furst & G. Storm, Eds. and Revisors.). New York: Doubleday, 1972. (Originally published, 1948.)

Higbee, K.L. *Your memory: How it works and how to improve it.* Englewood Cliffs, N.J.: Prentice-Hall, 1977.

Laird, D.A., & Laird, E.C. *Techniques for efficient remembering.* New York: McGraw-Hill, 1960.

Lorayne, H. *How to develop a super-power memory.* New York: Frederick Fell, 1957.

Lorayne, H. *Remembering people: The key to success.* Briarcliff Manor, N.Y.: Stein & Day, 1975.

Lorayne, H., & Lucas, J. *The memory book.* New York: Ballantine, 1974.

Rodale, J.I. *How to strengthen the memory.* Emaus, Pa.: Rodale Publications, 1937.

Roth, D.M. *Roth memory course.* Cleveland: Ralston Publishing, 1955.

Young, M.N., & Gibson, W.B. *How to develop an exceptional memory.* North Hollywood, Calif.: Wilshire Book Company, 1978.

Study techniques

These books suggest ways that you can learn to study more efficiently and in a more organized manner.

Apps, J.W. *Study skills: For those adults returning to school.* New York: McGraw-Hill, 1978.

Deese, J., & Deese, E.K. *How to study.* New York: McGraw-Hill, 1979.

Langan, J., & Nadell, J. *Doing well in college.* New York: McGraw-Hill, 1980.

History of mnemonic devices

The following is a list of books and articles that provide information about the history of mnemonic devices. You might also look up *mnemonics* in any one of the encyclopedias.

Crovitz, H.F. *Galton's walk.* New York: Harper & Row, 1970.

Hunter, I.M.L. Mnemonic systems and devices. *Science News,* 1956, *39,* 75-97.

Hunter, I.M.L. *Memory: Facts and fallacies,* Baltimore: Penguin, 1957.

Luria, A.R. *The mind of a mnemonist.* Chicago: Henry Regnery Company, 1976.

Rawles, R.E. The past and present of mnemotechny. In M. M. Gruneberg, P.E. Morris, & R.N. Sykes (Eds.), *Practical aspects of memory.* London: Academic Press, 1978.

Yates, F.A. *The art of memory.* London: Routledge & Kegan Paul, 1966.

Research on mnemonic devices

The results of research on mnemonic devices are scattered throughout the psychological and educational journals. The following is a list of books and articles that review and reference some of these results.

Bellezza, F.S. Mnemonic devices: Classification, characteristics, and criteria. *Review of Educational Research,* 1981, *51,* 247-275.

Higbee, K.L. *Your memory: How it works and how to improve it.* Englewood Cliffs, N.J.: Prentice-Hall, 1977.

Paivio, A. *Imagery and verbal processes.* New York: Holt, 1971.

Index